CHAUCER'S WORLD

A PICTORIAL COMPANION

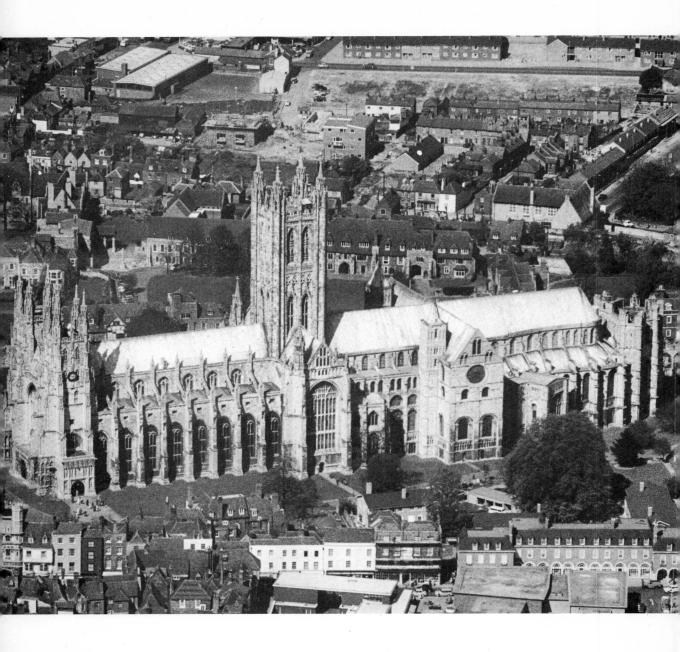

Canterbury Cathedral

CHAUCER'S WORLD
A PICTORIAL COMPANION

Photographs and Maps compiled
and introduced by

MAURICE HUSSEY

CAMBRIDGE
AT THE UNIVERSITY PRESS
1967

PUBLISHED BY
THE SYNDICS OF THE CAMBRIDGE UNIVERSITY PRESS
Bentley House, 200 Euston Road, London, N.W.1
American Branch: 32 East 57th Street, New York, N.Y. 10022

CAMBRIDGE UNIVERSITY PRESS
1967

This book is for

IAN BARKER

in recollection of our visit
to Rome at which we were greeted
by Pope John XXIII as pilgrims

Library of Congress Catalogue Card Number: 67-11523
PRINTED IN GREAT BRITAIN BY JARROLD AND SONS LTD, NORWICH

CONTENTS

Frontispiece: Canterbury Cathedral   *page* 2

Preface   6

Acknowledgements   7

1   Maps before the Journey   9

2   St Thomas of Canterbury   17

3   'Pilgrims were they All'   21

4   The Face of England   30

5   The Knight and his Company   37

6   The Regular Clergy   55

7   The Merchant   72

8   The Clerk   76

9   The Sergeant and his Company   87

10   The Gildsmen and their Cook   95

11   The Shipman   99

12   The Doctor of Physic   102

13   The Wife of Bath   110

14   The Militant Church   116

15   The Miller and the Reeve   131

16   Two Damned Souls   136

17   Two Final Introductions   142

18   Chaucer: Pilgrim-Poet   154

19   Pieter Brueghel   160

20   Taking it Further   164

List of Illustrations   168

PREFACE

This book has been compiled as a pictorial companion to *An Introduction to Chaucer* and the Chaucer Tales published in the same series. The reader for whom this book is intended is approaching the poet's work for the first time and attempting to assess it against the background of life and ideas current in the fourteenth century. Here, in order to achieve a reasonable balance of subjects, the text has been largely reduced to a series of background comments and precise criticisms of illustrations which have been chosen to cover both the concrete and the abstract features of Chaucer's period and work.

Although a number of the pictures are no more than records, some of them are works of art in their own right. Where possible they have been drawn from English sources and more attention has been paid to the dominating concepts of chivalry, religion, science and the like than to domestic trivialities. Architecture has not been fully represented because of the magnitude of the task and because of the availability of many authoritative books, not to mention the buildings themselves. Topics that might suit the folk-museum have been narrowed down and observations upon costume pared to the point at which they are part of the poet's particular vision of character.

It will quickly become plain to the reader that ideas discussed in one chapter are essential to the understanding of another. It is a disadvantage of the arrangement adopted for the book that full treatment of an idea may have to be delayed until a later page. This should be accepted as evidence of the fact that the 'sondry folk' are indeed the best possible selection of contemporary types, and that their main ideas are those which the reader has to discover for himself in the context of the poetry. There they will emerge as literary conventions and philosophical positions which Chaucer shares with his time and as indispensable to the process of understanding or criticizing the poetry. For, in the end, medieval literature is not 'about' pictures, bench-ends, misericords or gargoyles at all: it is about words, while Chaucer's words were central to living.

M. P. H.

Cambridge, May 1966

ACKNOWLEDGEMENTS

I am most deeply indebted to those who have helped me to find and allowed me to reproduce the illustrations which are the mainstay of this book. The list that follows gives details of the many courtesies extended to me by librarians, curators, photographers and publishers who have most kindly complied with my many requests. I should similarly acknowledge the kindness of my colleague Mr A. H. Carter who has drawn the maps in Chapter 1.

For a great deal of incidental advice and assistance I am most grateful for the presence of my friends James Winny, collaborator in *Selected Tales of Chaucer*, and Surendra Agarwala. The staff of the Cambridge University Press have given the greatest of assistance in the procuring of illustrations and in many other ways.

Frontispiece: Aerofilms Ltd; **1.** The Bodleian Library, Oxford; **5.** The British Museum; **6.** National Buildings Record; **7** (*a–l*) and **8** (*a–l*). Trinity College Library, Cambridge; **9, 10.** The British Museum; **11.** The University Library, Cambridge; **12.** National Buildings Record; **13, 14, 15.** The Committee for Aerial Photography, Cambridge University; **16, 17.** National Buildings Record; **18.** Henry E. Huntington Library and Art Gallery; **19.** The British Museum; **20.** The Fitzwilliam Museum, Cambridge; **21, 22.** The British Museum; **23.** Aerofilms and Aero Pictorial Ltd; **24, 25, 26.** The Committee for Aerial Photography, Cambridge University; **28.** National Buildings Record; **29.** Henry E. Huntington Library and Art Gallery; **30.** Photographie Giraudon; **31, 32.** The British Museum; **33.** Photographie Giraudon; **34, 35.** Henry E. Huntington Library and Art Gallery; **36.** The British Museum; **37.** Henry E. Huntington Library and Art Gallery; **38.** Photographie Giraudon; **39, 40.** The British Museum; **41.** John Rylands Library, Manchester; **43.** Director in Aerial Photography, Cambridge University; **44.** Royal Commission on Historical Monuments (England); **45.** Henry E. Huntington Library and Art Gallery; **46.** The Fitzwilliam Museum, Cambridge; **47.** Henry E. Huntington Library and Art Gallery; **48.** The Public Record Office; **49, 50.** The British Museum; **51.** Henry E. Huntington Library and Art Gallery; **52.** The British Museum; **53** (*a–i*). The University Library, Cambridge; **54.** The British Museum; **55.** Henry E. Huntington Library and Art Gallery; **56, 57.** The University Library, Cambridge; **58.** Henry E. Huntington Library and Art Gallery; **59.** The Fitzwilliam Museum, Cambridge; **60.** Henry E. Huntington Library and Art Gallery; **61.** Royal Commission on Historical Monuments (England); **62.** Public Record Office; **63.** The British Museum; **64.** G. Bernard Wood; **65.** Henry E. Huntington Library and Art Gallery;

66 (**a** and **b**). The British Museum; **67.** Henry E. Huntington Library and Art Gallery; **68, 69.** The British Museum; **70.** Henry E. Huntington Library and Art Gallery; **71.** Biblioteca Apostolica Vaticana; **72.** The British Museum; **73.** Courtauld Institute of Art; **74.** The Public Record Office; **75.** Henry E. Huntington Library and Art Gallery; **76.** National Buildings Record; **77, 78.** Prestel Verlag, München; **79.** Crown copyright: Ministry of Public Building and Works; **80.** Henry E. Huntington Library and Art Gallery; **81, 82.** National Buildings Record; **83.** G. L. Barnes; **84.** National Buildings Record; **85.** Surendra Agarwala; **86.** National Monuments Record (or Royal Commission on Historical Monuments (England)); **87.** University Library, Cambridge; **88.** National Buildings Record; **89, 90.** University Library, Cambridge; **91.** James Winny; **92.** National Buildings Record; **93, 94.** The British Museum; **95.** H. E. H. Library and Art Gallery; **96.** The Fitzwilliam Museum, Cambridge; **97.** Courtauld Institute of Art; **98.** H. E. H. Library and Art Gallery; **99.** The British Museum; **100.** Prestel Verlag, München; **101.** The British Museum; **102.** H. E. H Library and Art Gallery; **103.** Photographie Giraudon; **104.** H. E. H. Library and Art Gallery; **105.** Rev. W. Blathwayt; **106.** National Monuments Record; **107.** H. E. H. Library and Art Gallery; **108.** Photographie Giraudon; **109.** National Buildings Record; **110, 111, 112, 113.** The Walters Art Gallery, Baltimore; **114.** H. E. H. Library and Art Gallery; **115.** Fisher Scientific Corporation, Pittsburg; **116.** Prestel Verlag, München; **117.** Dr Joseph Needham, F.R.S.; **118.** H. E. H. Library and Art Gallery; **119.** Photographie Giraudon; **120.** Courtauld Institute of Art; **121.** The National Gallery; **122.** The Metropolitan Museum of Art, Rogers Fund, 1919; **123, 124.** Kunsthistorisches Museum, Vienna; **125.** Royal Commission on Historical Monuments (England).

1 *A Fourteenth-century Map of England: the Gough Map*

1 MAPS BEFORE THE JOURNEY

THE GOUGH MAP

From this reproduction of the best surviving fourteenth-century map of England (known as the *Gough Map*) the relative accuracy of the outline at least can be immediately appraised. Wales, Scotland and small pieces of the French coast seem to have been outside the cartographer's experience; it is offered as a contemporary account of the shape of the kingdom, and the sort of map Chaucer could have consulted, had he needed to do so.

The original is coloured with green and red, the lettering all orientated to the east, the rivers being far more prominent than the roads and presumably more reliable for transport. The unknown compiler used symbols for the forests and the towns, and his positioning of them is almost always accurate. All his thin red roads travel as the crow flies from town to town, ignoring contour and detour. From a fuller study of them it emerges that London already dominated the communications system, the main roads fanning out from the capital in all directions. The principal ones marked are: London to Devonshire; London to Bristol; London to St David's; London to Carlisle; London to Doncaster. The fact that there is no line going into East Anglia, one of the main centres of population and industry, is evidence that the work was left unfinished. It also emerges that the route from London to Canterbury (*Cantuar*) is complete as to towns, but the Pilgrim's Way, the route of most interest to readers of Chaucer, is not actually delineated. Thus, *Dertford, Graveshend, Rowchester, Sithinborn, Ospring, Fevarsham* and *Cantuar* are correctly designated. It is possible that the road itself was so poor that it was of use only to single horsemen and useless for commercial transport. One might have expected some recognition of the favourite English pilgrimage, since it seems reasonable to imagine that a member of the Church compiled it.

CHAUCER'S ENGLAND

The Kentish poet's loyalties towards the south-east are revealed in an instant. Knowing that corner of England well, he was anxious to feature it in his narratives; not knowing and possibly scorning the less densely populated northern counties, he made very little use of them. As a result England north of the Wash and the Avon is slighted, and what references there are carry little respect or credit.

Lincoln, the home of the boy saint, Hugh (*Prioress's Tale*), and *Hailes*, the Abbey celebrated for its specimen of the Holy Blood (*Pardoner's Tale*), get a single line apiece in the *Tales. Berwick* and *Hull* are figuratively introduced as the northernmost points of imaginary areas: the first area stretches down to *Ware* and is the one in which the

2 *Chaucer's England: a Modern Map showing all the Place-names mentioned by Chaucer, and, in lighter type, other Sites mentioned in this Book*

Pardoner has no peer; the latter reaches all the way to *Carthage* (Cartagena) and relates to the mastery of the Shipman. *Holderness*, a 'mershy contree', is made notorious for its grasping friars in the scurrilous *Summoner's Tale*.

Bawdeswell is the solitary outpost in Norfolk that needs to be mapped: it is the home of Oswald the Reeve. There is a long-standing legend that Chaucer himself came from King's Lynn. Had this been the case, one feels, he would have spoken more charitably about more northerly areas and not neglected his home county, which was an important one in the country's economy. *Cambridge*, with near-by *Trumpington* and its mill, are temporary residences for the two uncouth north-country undergraduates in the *Reeve's Tale*. Though at a spot only three miles away from college, they decide it is better not to risk the journey back by night—a comment on minor roads at this time— and there follows a series of mishaps for which any contrivance would have sufficed.

Orwell, the Suffolk anchorage facing Middelburgh in Holland, corresponds exactly to the modern port of Harwich facing The Hook. In the Middle Ages its importance to cloth traders was great, and both places are named in the portrait of the Merchant, who relied heavily upon export. *Dunmow* in Essex still offers a flitch of bacon for the couple that can swear they have passed a year and a day of matrimony without quarrel or other untoward incident. The Wife of Bath, who is a mistress of the cloth trade like the Merchant, reflects upon the misery of her first old spouses in these lines:

> The bacon was nat fet for hem, I trowe,
> That som men han in Essex at Dunmowe.

Ware, not far away, has already been mentioned. It was also the home of Roger the Cook.

There is no need to document the poet's use of *London*, in which he was born and brought up. *Westminster*, its twin city, contained Rouncival, a religious house which was the home of the Pardoner. Not far out in the fields lay *Stratford-atte-Bowe*, the home of the Prioress, which is now called Stratford East.

Oxford, westward along the Thames, is the home of two contrasting clerks. The Clerk of the *General Prologue*, rather bleak and colourless, is outbalanced by 'hende Nicholas', the astronomical student of the *Miller's Tale* who lodged at *Osney*, a suburb of the university town today, near the railway station. *Bath*, which evoked in the poet one of his finest responses, was quite certainly a place he had to visit on his professional work. He was Warden of *Petherton Forest* in Somerset, and when he journeyed there he was bound to pass Bath and find the small parish of St Michael, the cloth-manufacturing centre which was 'biside Bathe' where he found the inspiration for the Wife. For him she also represented the West Country cloth trade which would use either Bristol or *Dartmouth* for its exporting. From the latter, Chaucer writes, the Shipman plied his bark. It may be coincidence, but it seems that the *General Prologue* is directing our attention to the two cloth-making centres through the medium of carefully selected, almost symbolic characters. He might even have foreseen the later importance of *Sheffield*. It was there that the knife brandished by Simkin the miller in the *Reeve's Tale* was made: as early as the fourteenth century it had won its modern reputation for cutlery.

CHAUCER'S EUROPE

A medieval map of the world, known as *mappamundi*, gives no sense of the true shape of Europe. The most famous in England is too detailed to be reproduced and too complex and inaccurate in its outline to possess any other than curiosity value. It is to be found in Hereford Cathedral and should be visited and studied if possible. Its idiosyncrasy is that it places Jerusalem in the centre of the world and gives biblical places due prominence. It reveals that in the thirteenth century, when it was compiled, the outline of Europe was poorly understood. A quotation from the Book of Ezekiel explains the principle upon which it was constructed: 'This Jerusalem I have set in the

3 *Chaucer's Europe: a Modern Map showing all the Place-names mentioned by Chaucer*

midst of the nations round about her.' The centre of the map is reserved, therefore, for the city once called the navel of the world, the 'Jerusalem celestial' of the *Parson's Prologue*.

A map specially drawn to illuminate Chaucer's Europe, with the areas of his own travels readily deducible, is of more value to the modern reader. As with the English map, the outlying regions are more figures of speech than actual places. Thus, if the list of the cities visited by three travellers is omitted, there is a much narrower area left to be divided among the rest of *The Canterbury Tales*. The military campaigns of the Knight and Squire account for many entries between them, and the perambulations of the Wife of Bath add more, hinting of 'strange streams' that are not named. A common factor binds all these: they are outposts of Christian territory. The two men were employed on the frontiers of Christendom, defeating Moors, Turks and others who were menacing the faith; inside the boundaries they created, the pilgrim has safety to roam on pilgrimage.

The twin cores of Chaucer's Europe lie in the part of Northern France and Flanders nearest to England, and in Italy, both areas that he himself had visited. Italy is also the subject of a slightly tedious and repetitive geographical lecture in the *Clerk's Prologue*. Nor is Chaucer entirely accurate about the wanderings of the River Po. The companion edition of the *Clerk's Tale* contains another map of the area with further comments. In this connexion, it may be noted that the tales of the Clerk and the Merchant both relate to Lombardy. In one case, however, the world is dark and drab; in the other it is colourful and alive, as if prophetic of the world we know as Renaissance Italy. *Pisa* is a symbol of religious oppression in *The Canterbury Tales*, it is the scene of the imprisonment and torture of Count Ugolino which Chaucer translated from Dante. For Chaucer, Italy was the country of Dante, Boccaccio and Petrarch, and like so many other English poets he had great sympathy with Italy and gave it prominence in his writings. No country stirred his imagination more.

Artois, *Picardie* and *Boloigne* are three places in Northern Europe associated with two of Chaucer's three inveterate travellers. Exactly where Chaucer himself had travelled in the area is not known. *Ypres*, *Gaunt* (Ghent) and *Popering* are three centres of the clothing industry associated with the Wife in her capacity as a craftswoman. *La Rochelle* and *Bordeaux* are wine-centres, and among the Shipman's favourite ports of call. In the south of Spain is *Lepe*, another wine town mentioned in the *Pardoner's Tale*, while in the north is the tomb of St James of Compostella, with which the Wife was also acquainted.

The *Franklin's Tale* explains the place-names in Brittany, *Pedmark* being the shore from which the magician seemed to clear the dark rocks. What was once a major port is now Penmarch, an obscure village.

A number of classical place-names are added (such as *Thebes* and *Athens*, the world of the *Knight's Tale*): these reflect Chaucer's shadowy grasp of the ancient world. When some of his classical sites are studied it is found that they are visualized with medieval exteriors. The *Knight's Tale*, especially, is a case where Chaucer modernized the appearance and the customs to bring the past closer to the imagination of his own period. This, indeed, was what he usually contrived to do. He chose aspects of society which were most familiar to his audience; as a result, the map of Chaucer's Europe is a condensation of popular thought upon countries outside his own. He made his greatest effect by concentrating on areas with which he himself was familiar. In choosing places like *Palatie* (Balat), *Satalye* (Antalya), *Pruce* (Prussia), or *Lettow* (Lithuania) he was sending the imagination of his readers to the outposts of his civilization and beyond it to the world that was unconverted, unexplored and unmapped.

THE PILGRIM'S WAY

The small map shows the road from London to Canterbury which was normally followed by pilgrims. Known in early times as *Watling Street*, and originally a Roman road, it is still traceable on the way to the Cathedral or to Dover. In earlier days there were long stretches of road that divided woodlands and cornfields where today there are only buildings on either side. Those parts of the original way that still pass through open country possess little that is striking enough to show on a photograph. Its past rather than its present is what matters most.

Southwark was the normal starting-point for pilgrimages, though nobody is perfectly certain how individuals or small groups from all over the country were organized into suitable companies for a pilgrimage. It would seem possible that the Church added to its many other services that of the travel agency. It should be remembered that

4 *The Pilgrim's Way*

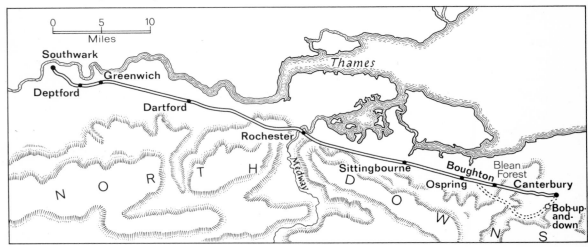

pilgrimages went out in all directions. Though none of them rivalled Canterbury, there were also visits to such places as Salisbury, Glastonbury, Walsingham and Hailes Abbey, to name but four.

Chaucer provides poetic signposts in the prologues and epilogues of the *Tales*, which continue the illusion of a journey. After a breather at the *Watering of St Thomas* (not shown because it is not identifiable) the pilgrims continued their story-telling and their journeying together. There is no attempt on the poet's part to relate the mileage to the length of narrative. The poet threw in signposts when he felt like it, as in

> Lo Depeford. . . .
> or
> Lo Grenewich, there many a shrewe is inne.

But he spares not a moment's attention for Blackheath, which had been the scene of Wat Tyler's camp during the Peasants' Revolt in 1381 and would have been good for a comment if he had been intending to describe the sights of the journey realistically. Nor does he spare a thought for Dartford, where pilgrims normally spent their first night out.

In the *Monk's Prologue* the company is found to be some thirty miles from the capital:

> Loe, Rouchestre stant heer faste by.

Having crossed the Medway they amble towards *Sittingbourne*, cited in the *Wife of Bath's Prologue*. The final leg of their journey we may presume started at *Ospring*. Not far from this point, and on the way through *Blean Forest*, Chaucer contrives for a newcomer to catch them up. He is the Canon's Yeoman who joins them and tells his tormented story. At *Boughton-under-Blee* there were two approaches to Canterbury open to travellers. They could keep straight ahead or turn south, their choice probably conditioned not so much by the length of the path as by the state of the road. Chaucer's final reference to his pilgrims' progress has not served to clarify which way the pilgrims would have taken. His lines are as follows:

> Woot ye nat where ther stant a litel toun
> Which that ycleped is Bobbe-up-and doun,
> Under the Blee, in Caunterbury weye?

If it is really a town it may be *Harbledown* on the direct road to the cathedral, but if it is the comical name that the reader goes by, then it may be Up-and-down field which is off the southern fork of the road. Neither place is more than a mile from the destination, but there is no indication in the text that the pilgrims finished the journey. Either by accident or design the pilgrimage was halted and the arrival in the city eternally postponed.

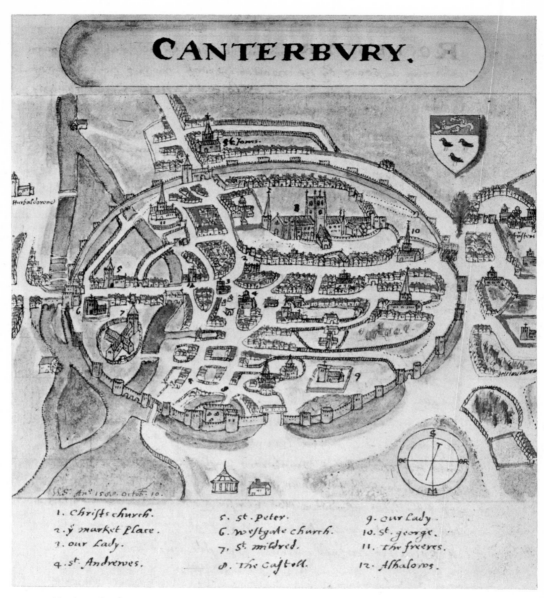

CANTERBVRY.

1. Christs church.
2. ỹ market place.
3. our Lady.
4. st Andrewes.

5. st peter.
6. westgate church.
7. st mildred.
8. the castell.

9. our Lady.
10. st george.
11. the freeres.
12. Alhalows.

5 *An old Plan of Canterbury*

MEDIEVAL CANTERBURY

The plan, dated 1588, is more strictly Christopher Marlowe's Canterbury than Chaucer's, but it seems unlikely that the city had changed a great deal in the intervening period. The whole area seems spacious, if haphazardly planned, with no hint of over-crowding.

In the broadest sense it is a circular walled city with a castle (foreground), a cathedral and a number of churches, both within and without the walls. As is shown (**5,** 11), there were friaries for Grey and Black Friars in the river sector of the city, while for a monastery it is only necessary to look towards the Cathedral, which was monastic in origin and still has the ruins of buildings needed for the social life of a religious community but not for the running of a secular cathedral. It will be seen too that only one of the towers at the west end was in place at the time the plan was drawn—the other had to wait until 1834 for its completion.

Since in each point of the compass there is a gate out of the city, the city presents a familiar pattern. From the West Gate runs Watling Street; from the North, the road to Margate; from the East, the road to Dover, while at the foot of the map is the road to Hastings. The river runs through the western sector, and the countryside is shown lying outside the gates especially at the head of the plan.

The Pilgrim's Way from Southampton enters the city near the West Gate. From Harbledown its route lay across country, along what is no more than a track today— for it did not persist to its destination in a straight line. In any case, it is not specifically marked on the plan.

THE CATHEDRAL

The aerial picture (frontispiece) shows the magnificent Cathedral as it is today. No cathedral is ever the work of a single life-span and it has often occurred that a segment of the building that pleased one generation was too small for the next and rebuilding was often undertaken even when portions had not fallen into disrepair. Canterbury was created during Norman times and then developed slowly. It was customary with all churches to provide an altar and a nave and then to extend in a westerly direction as funds permitted. The ideal in the English Gothic cathedral was to put up a high central tower and two more over the west door. One transept crossing the aisle turns the aerial view into a cross, and if it extended too far it would need a further cross-member to balance the first at a later stage in construction.

6 *The Martyrdom of St Thomas à Becket: a Roof boss*

The two transepts and the cruciform appearance seem overdramatized in this aerial view. The length of the nave is of particular interest. It may be attributed to the success of the pilgrimages and miracles of St Thomas that so much money was attracted to the Cathedral. With the offerings at Thomas's tomb (which is now completely destroyed) it was possible to build the new nave at the time *The Canterbury Tales* were being composed: they are exactly contemporary works of art.

The Cathedral stands 547 feet in length and 80 feet in height (apart from the towers) and is firmly planted in a cathedral close of grass, which is characteristic of most English cathedrals. It is recognized as a masterpiece of the Perpendicular style of building, one that was extensively practised in England although imported from the Continent. The proportion, height, light and spaciousness are all equally noticeable here, outside as well as inside, as they are at Westminster and Gloucester. All should be sought out by the inquiring reader, but in Canterbury above all the sense of Chaucer's period is maintained. Religious chivalry is to be found in the tomb of the Black Prince; Henry IV is buried there; and this was the goal sought out by so many people winding their way along bad roads and lanes from London into Kent in happy fellowship.

ST THOMAS À BECKET

'The hooly blisful martir' who is the patron-saint of Chaucer's poem, Thomas à Becket, was born in London in 1118. As Archbishop of Canterbury he became involved in prolonged quarrels with Henry II over matters concerning power and authority in

Church and State. At the height of these the King sent knights to Canterbury to kill the Archbishop on 29 December 1170. After the exceptionally short space of three years Thomas was canonized in Rome and became the most prominent of English saints, his relics venerated and visited to an unprecedented degree. Nothing is today to be seen of the splendours of the shrine, which was dismantled at the Reformation, but the extent and beauty of the entire building owe much to the wealth it accumulated from hosts of pilgrims who came to seek him out precisely in the terms Chaucer gives.

In our own day the murder of Becket has attracted the art of dramatists such as Jean Anouilh and T. S. Eliot, but in the Middle Ages the natural medium was Church art. The very fine fourteenth-century roof boss in Exeter Cathedral illustrated here (**6**) gives an indication of the beauty of the medium handled by unknown craftsmen in churches and cathedrals up and down the country.

Roof bosses were sometimes carved at the intersection-point of cross-beams in the church vault. Sometimes heraldic, floral or other decorative designs would be executed, but the most interesting ones show a range of dramatic subjects from history and mythology. In other churches it was customary to place angels on small projecting platforms (known as hammer-beams) which gave the impression of their hovering over the nave about to descend. Bosses were left intact at the Reformation (while statues and other decorations at floor-level were mutilated or destroyed) because they could not easily be reached. One of the discoveries of the present century has been the telephotographic lens by which we can know again the riches hidden in high roofs.[1]

In this example (for another see p. 125) the task is to group so many people on one small spherical carving. The four knights, Fitz-Urse, de Tracey, de Morville and le Breton, crowd behind the Archbishop in the foreground, while almost half the area is given to the clerk named Grimm. He is trying to shield the martyr and hinting with his crucifix at a comparison with the death of Christ on the Cross. Facial expressions, hair-styles and the folds of the clothing are most carefully chiselled. Since this example was made in Chaucer's lifetime the armour reflects the fourteenth century. There is, in fact, no attempt to reconstruct a historical scene, since for so many people the martyrdom of the prominent English Saint had some of the eternal contemporaneity of the crucial events in the New Testament, which were always made to fit into the period of any artist who chose to paint them, so as to relate them to the present. The martyrdom of St Thomas was eternally present as long as it was commemorated by regular pilgrimages.

[1] C. J. P. Cave, *Roof Bosses in Medieval Churches* is an indispensable guide to this topic and offers a very large number of photographs.

7 *Months of the Year.* (a) *January, drinking by the fire.* (b) *February, digging in the fields and setting seed.* (c) *March, pruning vines.* (d) *April, carrying flowering branch.* (e) *May, hawking.* (f) *June, mowing the hay.* (g) *July, cutting the corn with a sickle.* (h) *August, threshing with a flail.* (i) *September, picking grapes.* (j) *October, sowing winter corn.* (k) *November, gathering acorns to feed the pigs.* (l) *December, pig-killing*

THE CALENDAR AND THE ZODIAC

The unparalleled piece of springtime poetry that opens the *General Prologue* barely needs reference to the appropriate March and April scenes from the series collected here. By itself the verse forces the reader to respond to the quickening of the air and under the ground. Philosophically, it typifies the resurgence of the *vegetative soul* in the plants, the *animal soul* in the birds, and the *human soul* in mankind, seeking a spiritual pathway and undertaking a pilgrimage along it. For the lower order of creation it is a mating-drive, but for mankind it is an elevation to the plane of eternity.

> Whan that Aprill with his shoures soote
> The droghte of March hath perced to the roote,
> And bathed every veine in swich licour
> Of which vertu engendred is the flour;
> Whan Zephirus eek with his sweete breeth
> Inspired hath in every holt and heeth
> The tendre croppes, and the yonge sonne
> Hath in the Ram his halve cours yronne,
> And smale foweles maken melodie,
> That slepen al the night with open ye
> (So priketh hem nature in hir corages);
> Thanne longen folk to goon on pilgrimages.

Those who owned but one book in the Middle Ages might well have had a prayer-book faced by a perpetual calendar, divided into twelve month-pages. If they were rich enough they would have these illuminated. A modest example of such work is the volume in the library of Trinity College, Cambridge, from which this series of minia-tures has been taken (**7**). Alongside it one could place images carved in wood and stone and glassed in windows all over Europe. The finest of all calendars is that provided for the Duc de Berri by Pol de Limbourg and his two brothers from which the May, December and February pages are reprinted in this book (**30, 33, 108**) on pp. 49, 53 and 143.

There is general agreement upon the signs of the zodiac for any given date and, as will become evident later, much depended upon them. There was much less agreement, however, on the dating of different agricultural tasks. An obvious source of this lack of unanimity is in the differences of climate in different countries that employed pictorial representations. As an indication of a different order of labours look at the passage which follows. The miniatures themselves (**8**) pose no problem. A realism is

THE SIGNS OF THE ZODIAC AND THEIR ASSOCIATIONS

Temperament	Humour	Element	Colour	Condition	Quality	Age	Season	Wind	Sign of Zodiac	Part of Body
Sanguine	Blood	Air	Red	Liquid	Hot-moist	Childhood	Spring	South	ARIES TAURUS GEMINI	Head Neck Shoulder
Choleric	Yellow Bile	Fire	Yellow	Gaseous	Hot-dry	Youth	Summer	East	CANCER LEO VIRGO	Upper Body
Melancholic	Black Bile	Earth	Black	Dense	Cold-dry	Maturity	Autumn	North	LIBRA SCORPIO SAGITTARIUS	Lower Body
Phlegmatic	Phlegm	Water	White	Solid	Cold-Moist	Old Age	Winter	West	CAPRICORNUS AQUARIUS PISCES	Thigh Knee Foot

evident in them and the attractive features of the workers find their correspondence in the sympathetic treatment of the animals. It will, in fact, be seen throughout this book that animals are given their place in the scheme of things, and are well drawn and painted. Philosophically, this is a manifestation of what was called *haeccitas* ('thisness'), a belief in the validity of all orders of creation as parts of the divine plan, challenging compassion and understanding and not casual patronage.

> By thys fyre I warme my handys;
> And with my spade I delfe[1] my landys.
> Here I sette my thynge[2] to sprynge;
> And here I here the fowlis synge.
> I am as lyght as byrde in bowe.
> And I wede my corne well i-now,
> With my sythe my mede[3] I mawe;[4]
> And here I shere my corne full lowe.
> With my flayll I erne my brede;
> And here I sawe[5] my whete so rede.
> At Martynemasse I kylle my swyne;
> And at Cristesmasse I drynke red wine.

The final passage is a Chaucerian extension of the zodiac sequence. It comes from the description of a winter journey in the *Franklin's Tale* and forms a counterbalance to the well-known opening paragraph. In a way it is this passage that most resembles the pictorial tradition, embracing the orders of creation once more, and might well be seen as rounding the year off in perfect order and harmony.

[1] dig.   [2] crop.   [3] meadow.   [4] mow.   [5] sow.

8 *Signs of the Zodiac.* (a) *Aquarius, the water-carrier.* (b) *Pisces, the fishes.* (c) *Aries, the ram.* (d) *Taurus, the bull.* (e) *Gemini, the twins.* (f) *Cancer, the crab.* (g) *Leo, the lion.* (h) *Virgo, the virgin.* (i) *Libra, the balance.* (j) *Scorpio, the scorpion.* (k) *Sagittarius, the archer.* (l) *Capricorn, the goat*

9 *The Three Estates*

And this was, as thise bookes me remembre,
The colde, frosty seson of Decembre.
 Phebus wax old, and hewed lyk laton,[1]
That in his hoote declinacion
Shoon as the burned gold with stremes brighte;
But now in Capricorn adoun he lighte,
Where as he shoon[2] ful pale, I dar wel seyn.
The bittre frostes, with the sleet and reyn,
Destroyed hath the grene in every yerd.[3]
Janus sit by the fyr, with double berd,
And drinketh of his bugle horn the wyn;
Biforn him stant brawen[4] of the tusked swyn,
And 'Nowel' crieth every lusty man.

THE THREE ESTATES

All who appreciate the representativeness of that company alleged to have left the Tabard Inn in Southwark on a legendary April day will regret that no contemporary artist was engaged to give a group portrait of them before they left.

 The first illustration (**9**), from the thirteenth century, with its awkward figures, lacks all sense of Chaucerian individuality, but it is pointing in the right direction. The three characters are drawn from the branches of feudal society—the Knight, the Priest and the Labourer. In Latin writings they were termed *Bellator* (war-maker), *Orator*

[1] brass. [2] shone. [3] garden. [4] brawn.

10 *A Group of Fifteenth-century Pilgrims*

(offerer of prayer) and *Laborator* (ploughman), and from a French tradition the idea was brought into England. The three find expression in the foundations of the British governmental system: Lords Temporal, Lords Spiritual and the Commons. With an eye avid for complexity the preacher Wiclif likened them to the Father, the Son and the Holy Spirit.

A further illustration of the rigidity of the fixed medieval society is to hand in any chess-set. Chaucer uses the image of chess in *The Book of the Duchess* but does not revert to it in *The Canterbury Tales.* Even so, another writer, Jacobus de Cessolis, followed up the feudal implications of the game, and wrote his *Chess Book* based upon it. In his interpretation—which was widely shared—the gentry are protected by quite distinct and individual pawns. Thus, in the back row the King and Queen, together with Bishop, Knight and Castle (or the royal bailiff who occupied it) symbolize the different political, military and ecclesiastical estates, or moves, laid down by universal agreement. The pawns have their subsidiary roles, equally undeviating. The correct interpretation of the pawns makes them look more and more like Canterbury Pilgrims : they were farmers, smiths, clerks, merchants, physicians, tavern-keepers, guards and custom officials, rioters and outlaws.

The small pilgrim group (**10**) was painted in the fifteenth century. A man who may be the Knight is being addressed by the Franklin or the Sergeant of the Law. Friar (with cowl) and Monk hold the centre, while a young man, too nondescript in his clothes for a convincing Squire, rides at the right-hand side. The solitary figure in the background

11 *Pilgrims leaving Southwark from the Tabard Inn*

is well in accordance with the secretiveness of the Merchant. There the cavalcade ends, leaving behind the white crenellated walls of London. It is a theory, however, that the poet Lydgate is one of the riders (since the painting is to be found in a manuscript of his *Troy Book*), but the general pattern allows still of the above interpretation.

The third picture (11) is taken from an eighteenth-century edition of Chaucer but is allegedly based on older drawings of the region of Southwark. The pilgrims are leaving the series of wooden buildings at a fair canter. It is in general terms a probable depiction of the region of the Tabard, but since there was a fire in the area towards the end of the seventeenth century there may be no direct observation behind this engraving. It is known that there were many pilgrim inns in the borough: 'George', 'Hart', 'King's Head' and 'Queen's Head' were recorded in Elizabethan times. All ale-houses in the Middle Ages used a stake projecting from the upper storey across the road as a sign. In this scene it has been civilized and made into a signboard which stretches all the way across the road. However, it seems that a shield rather than a tabard is depicted on its board.

PILGRIM INNS

For a true picture of a pilgrim inn we move across England to Glastonbury. This pilgrimage-centre was associated with the legends of King Arthur, St Patrick and Joseph of Arimathea, who is said to have come to England with the Holy Grail, or chalice, which had been used to transport the blood of Christ. The pilgrimage was of great

12 *The George Inn, Glastonbury*

importance and the George Inn (**12**) was developed from the monastery guest-house and built in its present form in 1475. It remains the finest example in England.

This 'Old Pilgrimmes Inne' is an example of a Late Gothic style. It is still castellated as was the custom with many non-military buildings, and in the manner of the medieval ale-house, it has a projecting post for the signboard which would in the past have been the ale-stake. One can divide the individual floors and windows in two ways: as a vertically stressed structure with the window-frames acting as props to the floors above, or as an extended grid pattern in which rectangles dominate. In that case, the dividing-line is the door-post. On one side is a large bay which runs all the way down the house and on the other is a pattern of six sections (five of window and one of flattened door) each one individually treated with arched or rounded windows set in rectangular window-frames.

The total effect is of immense solidity, and of magnificent preservation. Among the smaller details of the façade note the shields over the doorway identifying the resident, the repetitions of the Cross of St George and the niches, now devoid of saints. It reminds the viewer occasionally of the church architecture out of which it sprang, yet it would have no space for the soaring lines of church windows. It has become a town building in which a basically simple structure has been turned from a single flat surface into a variety of smaller ones.

THE PORTRAIT MINIATURES

A word is essential about the portrait miniatures of pilgrims that appear frequently in this book. The most celebrated and complete series of such portraits of Chaucer's pilgrims comes from the Ellesmere MS, written and decorated in the early years of the fifteenth century and now in the Huntington Library in the U.S.A. It seems that the artists have taken pains to verify the styles of clothing, which would not have been difficult at the time when they were working. They were equally careful about the equine portraits. Thus, although they were drawn a decade or two after the poet's death, he would have recognized his own intentions in the majority of them.

Their place in the MS (which is named after the collector and not the scribe) is to form headings to the separate *Tales* and not to the portraits in the *General Prologue*. This accounts for the absence of those pilgrims who do not tell a tale, such as the Squire's Yeoman; it also accounts for the apparent importance of the Second Nun and the Nun's Priest who are only shadowy figures in the opening poem, and for the inclusion of the Canon's Yeoman, the last-minute interloper who tells one of the late *Tales*.

A glance at the series reveals the artist's main problem: it is the spatial relation of horse and rider. In many cases it is poorly managed, the horses seeming stunted in growth and in one case rather like a bear. Since later comments will concern the riders only it may be worth a moment to show social stratification from the horses alone, as an immediate start in the social placing of the riders. The Knight's mount is different from the Clerk's, as would befit the completely contrasting riders. The first is a mettlesome warhorse, branded with a shape that resembles the letter *M*. This was customary with the German cavalry horses of the period. The studs on the thongs of the crupper, and the sturdier ones on the shoes, give the modern reader a hint of what the best horses were wearing during the period. How rough and wild the horse could then be is apparent in the tougher ones ridden by the Shipman and the Summoner.

Although the Franklin's mount is not pretentious, the Merchant's, which is probably of Arab extraction and rises in a posture called courbetting (or curvetting) as does the Squire's, suggests the social aspiration and possibly the travels of the rider. The bells that jingled in the wind to the pleasant distraction of the Monk are clear from the portrait; while it is the horse and not the Pardoner who carries the sack of relics. A final point concerns the ladies of the group. The religious ride side-saddle, while the Wife, with her legs deep in a foot-mantle, is in the more manœuvrable position astride, and with a whip in her hand, which also symbolizes her control over the male sex.

One or two other portraits of the pilgrims exist, including a far superior Wife of Bath, but there is no rival to the Ellesmere pictures. In 1491 appeared the first printed edition of the *Tales*, with woodcuts. Once more they are incomplete, the style is that of the century of their creation, and spoiled by the use of the same block to depict more than one person. It is perhaps surprising, considering the popularity of the poem, that more manuscripts were not illuminated in the fourteenth and fifteenth centuries. Even more surprising and regrettable is the allied fact that there are no illustrations of the tales themselves.

VILLAGES

Village life, indoors and out, lies at the heart of much of Chaucer's poetry and any collection of medieval secular illuminations will inevitably yield pictorial information upon a land that was largely agricultural. As a whole, England was then much more deeply wooded than now, and between the woods and the marshes and in clearings were small communities of people. Dwellings from which back paths led down to moorlands or to cultivated fields dotted the landscape, and stood up to show that human order was prevailing out of the wildness of nature. Where the roads were little more than tracks it was dangerous to roam at night because of the presence of prowling thieves, foxes and wolves.

Villages grew up in accordance with two main patterns: either formed round a green in front of a church or strung out along a road. In each case it was essential to provide premises for an ale-house, a carpenter, one or two other shops and workshops, an inn and a church, and siting for cottages.

The fields for cultivation often lay between the cottages and the moorlands and were grouped round the village on either side of a lane or street. It was not thought necessary to produce more than the community itself could use, and the process of bringing additional fields into cultivation was slow. The villagers grew only what was necessary for life: wheat, barley, rye, oats, peas and beans. The fields belonged either to the manor, or to the tenants as a group, and were then divided into small strips so that each family should have an equal share of all the land possessed in common. The unreclaimed land was left for animal grazing and was again held in common until it was put under the plough. Even then it was shared out with the utmost fairness.

The normal method was to rotate the crops sown. One field would be used for a cereal crop, a second for hay or root vegetables, while the third was left fallow for grazing and brought back into the cycle after a year's rest. In this method no land would be impoverished or eroded through over-cultivation. It also meant that the ploughing was a good deal harder when the fallow field had to be brought back to cropping. These difficulties are multiplied when it is seen that each strip (between six and twelve yards wide), the responsibility of a single family, had to be ploughed by members of that family. Paths or banks between the different strips made it impossible for the whole field to be put under the furrow at one time.

At some time during the later Middle Ages most villages were forced to accommodate themselves to sheep-farming, which completely altered the face of the land. The depopulation of the countryside caused by the Black Death and the slow drift to the

13 *Great Gidding*

towns left the manors too short-handed to work all the fields with necessary care. At this moment of labour shortage the lord had to decide whether or not to amalgamate the strips and enclose the fields with bushes and trees. A few shepherds could serve the demands of thousands of sheep, whereas the entire village was needed for the continuous cultivation of arable land. As men were dispossessed and drifted away there were many complaints that the sheep had replaced and eaten up the men's prospects, but it became quickly apparent that the economic survival of the country was made the more remarkable after the Black Death by the wool and cloth industries for which England was famous throughout the Continent.

The villages in the aerial photographs develop some of the themes already stated. If we walk through one of the villages it is only the modern surface that we see, where from the air the whole pattern is shown to have changed little in six or seven hundred years.

Great Gidding in Huntingdonshire (**13**) is in the heart of the countryside, having as its neighbours Little Gidding and Steeple Gidding. In the Middle Ages there was arable farming, but from the sixteenth century more space was monopolized by pasture-land.

Since that time the land-utilization has changed little. Along the main street are some fifty houses. Each house once had, and most still have, its own 'toft' or small-holding behind it. A hedge now runs along joining the ends of the tofts. This was called the 'back lane', and villagers could walk along it to their strips of land in the adjoining fields. Though there is little of it, the village could be said to show fairly regular planning. The church is on a small rise and not approached by a roadway. Otherwise, the main street contains an inn, a shop or two, a chapel, a village hall and a number of houses and farm-buildings. It is not possible or necessary to distinguish all these features from the photograph. It will be seen that there is evidence of a more scattered type of modern village-planning at the base of the photograph, encroaching on the old green at the crossroads, though everything else conforms to the pattern of the straight-line village. What the photograph does not tell, and where it may even prove misleading, is the overall size. It takes about two minutes on foot to cover the entire area in the photograph, and so it must always have been since the time of the first church in the thirteenth century and the disused windmill from the same period (which is not visible in the picture).

If Great Gidding is considered to be typical of the overall pattern of a medieval village, *Padbury* in Buckinghamshire (**14**) enables still more of the actual texture to be observed.

14 *Padbury*

15 *Braunton*

The aerial camera picks out the ridges and furrows of the medieval strip holdings. The modern hedges cut right across them. The trees in the centre of the field—not, as might be expected, round the boundaries—have always been obstacles for the plough, as the ground contour shows. The difference between the fields on either side of the lane is due to the changes in soil and drainage that forced itself upon the cultivators and left their permanent mark.

Braunton in Devon is unusual in retaining its open fields and adhering to them right up to the present day, with few of the hedges imposed by modern enclosure. Here it is the contrasting colours of the different crops that strike the eye (**15**). Each of the large colour strips was itself sub-divided into family holdings. Note the evidence of the strip system that still remains in the narrower bands of colour. The fields have remained devoid of trees as boundaries or wind-breaks and can have changed little since 1324 when the village was first surveyed.

16 *Fourteenth-century Cottage in Hagbourne, Berkshire*

Village homes were often huts of wood, clay, stone, mud, straw or turf. Few families could afford more than one storey because an upper storey called for a stronger structure. All they owned was a triangular or tent-shaped skeleton upon a firm base and it is not surprising that none of these has survived.

The two-storeyed cottage in Fig. **16** has now disappeared altogether and that in Fig. **17** has been renovated. The first was in Hagbourne in Berkshire, the second in Didbrook in Gloucester. They are typical timber-framed buildings, rough but extremely strong, and so have lasted down the centuries from the fourteenth, when they were built. Both show the triangular timber, the *cruck*, which is the load-bearing part of the structure, with an outer beam on each side whose function is to carry the roof-beams clear of the main members although they continue to bear weight. Windows and doors can only be placed within or immediately below longitudinal timbers since the lath-and-plaster walls are too weak to hold them. The thick straw thatch insulates the first building well. Although they are both clumsy in their handling of the wood skeleton, they have been durable. The cottage in Fig. **17** shows evident rebuilding in stone on the right-hand side.

Very few cottages earlier than 1500 exist in England today, although more modern buildings may have an older core. In that case it fails to give the note of appropriate antiquity that belongs to the period when a cottage was a triumph of hard carpentry, often by an owner-occupier.

17 *Fourteenth-century Cottage in Didbrook, Gloucestershire*

TOWNS

Because the timeless agent, the land, is less prominently displayed in the town it is more difficult to arrive at a general pictorial concept for the medieval city. The town of Caernarvon (**27**) gives a pattern that is common enough, with a fortress and a regular grid-pattern of streets, but not all medieval towns were like this. Some were protected by nothing better than a ditch and a rampart.

Towns could only prove attractive to newcomers from the diminishing villages if there they were to be kept safe and given more amenities than they had previously enjoyed. Thus, a market place is a good deal more than it may seem. In the main square there is room for a market, a commercial centre, a town hall, space for theatrical and even sporting events. Churches and, later on, large inns, hospitals and schools were all essential to the community and were, in addition, feasts for the eye, being built with a high level of taste. There had to be room for rows of shops, either in arcades or in lines throughout the most approachable parts of the town. Apartments overhead often 'jettied' out over the ground floor. In the upper apartments the family and sometimes workmen lived; in the lower apartments there would be a shop or a workshop. Because glass was for long a rarity there were no large shop-windows and the sign over the door was often more important as a means of identification than other evidence of the work carried on. In every way the local communities had to respond to the demand for communal living and compensate by public action for the lack of privacy experienced in most quarters. Out of that community spirit grew the gilds, the annual dramatic presentations and many other expressions of a corporate identity such as we ourselves, with vastly superior accommodation and facilities, largely lack.

Not all the towns were rectangular, even though this is the most logical assertion of the planning concept. Many towns, and the map (5) shows that Canterbury was one, were dotted with irregularly placed buildings, so dispersed because of the limits of building plots. It also happened that empty spaces were left, uneconomically, because no developer had taken up the option of land-purchase.

The reader able to visit such a city as York or Oxford will find the twisting streets of the medieval world still preserved there. At Lavenham, in Suffolk, a small medieval town remarkable for its concentration of sixteenth-century buildings, none of the main lines of development is straight and rectangular. In that town, it is true, there are one or two houses from Chaucer's century, but the general effect is of a slightly later period. Most towns have changed a great deal more as Elizabethan man, in turn, gave way to Georgian man and then to the Victorian lover of restoration when much was destroyed or hidden. Somewhere under a Georgian façade there may be a medieval chamber, or in another place the back view may be much older and more crooked than the front, which has been tidied and straightened up. Old exposed timbering gives strength to a town view but later builders preferred gracefulness and delicacy. To see a row of old cruck-houses with upper floors jettying out across the street so that owners may shake hands from upstairs windows is now rare in England. But even if it is discovered, it will have to be remembered that a town is not a single street, or a few odd buildings here and there; it is a community and a frame of mind as well. Medieval planners expressed the preconceptions of their time in their work and it is this quality that is impossible to illustrate today from pictures.

18 *The Knight*

THE KNIGHT

Chaucer's Knight will always be admired as an epitome of chivalric virtues, but there are many equals in the courtly literature of the period. The poem *Sir Gawain and the Green Knight*, for instance, offered a more searching analysis of the moral basis of the code of chivalry.

It was possible, as historians have proved, for a fourteenth-century knight to have been present in all the campaigns listed so freely in Chaucer's text, but there is no need to believe this literally: it is only poetically true. The Ellesmere illustrator has caught the Knight in a different pose. Chaucer suggests that he has come directly back from battle, his clothes still stained with rust from his armour, to offer a pilgrimage in return for his safety. Yet in this portrait he seems already a country gentleman and accustomed to such a role (**18**). The long toes of his hose dangle far below his spurs and all that he shows of his arms and armour is his gauntlet gloves and dagger. The hat is one of the fashionable long-tailed type known as the *liripipe*.

The Ellesmere Knight is a gentleman enjoying his leisure in times of peace. Not the knight in full armour, but the one who has to tell a very long tale and says self-consciously of his work as a narrator:

I have, God woot, a large feeld to ere

as if brandishing his role as farmer at his listeners.

For the armoured knight look at the other illustrations in this chapter. Each small piece of armour acquired a name during the Middle Ages but there was occasionally some difference of opinion on the terminology to be used. It is unnecessary to develop here the entire vocabulary. The main parts of a suit of armour are as follows: the *helm* covering the head; the movable *visor* above the *beaver*, which covered the face; the *cuirass* protecting the chest; *cuisses* and *greaves* fitting down the leg and *rerebrace* and *vambrace* descending the arm. Horses, too, had equally powerful protection in battle array. Their heads were hidden in *chamfrons* with *crinets* on the neck and *peytrals* on the breast.

There has been much discussion on the weight of armour, and Mr Ewart Oakeshott, author of *The Knight and his Armour*, has demonstrated to me that a full suit of armour was not a complete bar to movement although it discouraged prolonged and rapid walking. Well made, a suit of armour allowed reasonable freedom: even the vast suit

19 *Sir Geoffrey Luttrell in Armour*

20 *Storming a Castle*

made for the fattest of all knights, Henry VIII, presumably allowed its occupant to move. The idea perpetuated by the film of *Henry V*, with knights needing cranes to deposit them on horseback, turns out to be a piece of ludicrous inaccuracy in a film which contains art work of great delicacy and perception.

The arming of Sir Geoffrey Luttrell (1276–1345) found in the famous Luttrell Psalter is a useful pictorial accompaniment at this point (**19**). He is having handed to him a helmet with its heraldic device attached to it and a lance with its gonfalon or pennon. The Luttrell arms which are repeated on helmet, pennon, pauldron (on shoulder), surcoat, saddle, horse's embroidered surcoat, shield and headpiece as well as on the two ladies' dresses, consist of a bend with six martlets (heraldic birds without legs) in silver on an azure background. The Knight is here being equipped by the two sorrowful ladies (who look, with oval faces, people from the world of earlier medieval art) for an expedition to France and one cannot imagine any knight in the battle who displayed his pride of ancestry more obviously.

The illustration of siege warfare (**20**) shows how the turrets were used for defence and how ladders were brought up to storm the walls. When this method was not practicable, catapults, battering-rams or siege-towers were moved into position. If these failed, miners might dig pits and hack away at the foundations, though in the process they were easy targets for boiling oil and bran from above.

The picture of the knights and their sovereign (**21**) shows a wide variety of head-gear and an excessive number of well-shod hooves somewhat out of perspective. Note again the heraldic shields and pennons.

In order to acquire skill and keep in combat-training it was the practice to joust or participate in mock-battles called tournaments. These were formal occasions with roughly fifty contestants a side all contributing towards a vast piece of practical chivalric education with highly developed rules of procedure. In 1390, for instance, an elaborate one was mounted at Smithfield, which Chaucer may well have witnessed: 'Those Knights being in the king's party had their armour and apparrell garnished with white Hartes and Crownes of gold about the Harts necks [the personal emblem of Richard II, as we shall see on p. 159] and so they came riding through the streets of London to

21 *Riding with the King*

22 *Jousting*

Smithfield with a great number of trumpets and other instruments of musicks before them.' Richard loved these exhibitions and Chaucer, almost appropriately, transferred one into Ancient Greece in the *Knight's Tale*. Complete records of tournaments, however, conjure up more colourful events than those in Chaucer's poetry.

Jousting was rather more sedate, and this took the place of the tournament in later years. In this illustration (**22**) the white knight shows the three leopards of England on his shield, his shoulder and his horse's surcoat. He has aimed at his opponent's helm and knocked it off. At his own helm he wears a sleeve, perhaps given him by some lady, in whose honour he fights, as a favour. Neither horse is strongly protected, as this is not essential; and one of them has bells like those upon the Monk's mount. The chain-mail of the Oriental fighter is revealed and his shield is emblazoned with the cartoon of a native ruler or a heathen god.

Gervase Mathew[1] has remarked of knighthood in Chaucer's day that it sprang from a 'class society in which personal relationships held primary importance and in which the emotional content is provided by a romantic, perhaps rather adolescent conception of personal loyalty, friendship and adventure.'

CASTLES

The relatively modest social standing of Chaucer's Knight would have excluded him from ownership of one of the greatest of royal castles that are still to be seen in England as memorials of days of civil war, when thick fortifications were in demand more against Scottish or Welsh rebels than against foreign invaders from the Continent.

[1] In 'Ideals of Knighthood', in *Studies . . . presented to F. M. Powicke* (1948).

23 *Stokesay Castle*

A Knight of this class might have owned such a manor as Stokesay Castle in Shropshire (**23**) built in the 1270s and 1280s as a lightly fortified manor-house. It was possibly too far from the Welsh border to make elaborate fortifications necessary, but its state of preservation is good and in this excellent photograph a great number of the features common to all castles can be speedily identified. The entire area inside the walls is known as the *bailey*, the flat courtyard from which the buildings and the well stand out. Outside the walls the present sunken garden is in fact the castle *moat* which encircled the entire area and cut off the manor in watery isolation.

The strength of any castle resided in its *keep* which might have been placed either in the centre of rings of fortification or in the walls so as to be a look-out point as well as a stronghold. Stokesay Keep is octagonal and supported, like the Hall, by *buttresses*. The *parapet* at the head allows men to walk round as watchmen without exposing themselves to enemies on the ground. On each face of the octagon is a break in the wall known as a *machicolation* from which weapons were aimed, while below the parapet on the second floor is a long slit window designed for the arms of the archer. A small separate bridge leads to the keep. When all other parts of a castle were taken, the defenders retired into the keep and prepared to stand a siege.

Many medieval castles retain their fortified *gatehouses* from which a *drawbridge* could be let down and taken up at need. Stokesay has a domestic timbered building in black and white, the patterning repeated in the North Tower and popular throughout the counties on the Welsh border of England. In days of tough necessity there was no room for such decorative beauty on an exposed part like a gatehouse. Today it has only a wooden gate blocking the entrance; this is plainly insufficient to hold back a determined armed force.

The largest part of the castle is the Hall. The ground-level entrance was intended for the owners, while the steps at the south end near the keep lead to a private room known as the *solar*. Domestic quarters in the Middle Ages would have been sparsely furnished, the only splashes of colour being tapestries, armour, antlers and commemorative banners. The high table on its dais across the top end looked the length of the hall to an open fire located underneath the northern chimney. In some halls there was also a minstrel's gallery above. The width of the windows tells the onlooker that there was no danger from weapons, and their height gives an external impression of the height of the single room within. Only at the north end is there evidence of a second floor in use for bedrooms.

A pathway forms a boundary to the whole manor and leads on into the churchyard, to the church itself, and on finally to the rest of the neighbouring hamlet.

For one moment, a much earlier site can be recalled. It shows the remains of a fortification built by William the Conqueror, of whom the *Anglo-Saxon Chronicle* said: 'Castles he caused to be made, and poor men to be greatly oppressed.' Even before the celebrated Battle of Hastings in 1066 he began building a castle there, a scene which is portrayed on the famous Bayeux Tapestry.

Old Sarum (**24**) had been a Roman stronghold, and William the Conqueror's plan was to ensure the maximum protection for his keep by placing it inside concentric mounds and moats. Thus firmly entrenched, the hill fort was impregnable, and within its walls there grew up a crowded city. In the thirteenth century the inhabitants began to desert it, for what precise reason we do not know, and established a new and beautifully geometrically patterned city called New Sarum, or Salisbury. In Chaucer's day the

24 *Old Sarum*

desertion was not complete, but in our picture the scene is of an excavation and a ruin from which the defensive elements are easily traced. Note the cross-shaped outlines of the old cathedral: the slightly raised cloister near the eastern end, and a chapter-house of which a few stones still stand. What is confused from the ground, the only level at which the builder saw it, is much clearer from the air and an aerial photograph can reveal things hidden to common sight. Note the central keep, with its moat, and its own *motte* or mound.

The Warkworth picture shows a small castle in the context of field and town (**25**). The ring wall has tower defences all round its perimeter; it is not protecting a central keep as at Old Sarum. The fortified main gateway leads off to the moors, while the large castle buildings erected at the rear in 1400 give a view of the main street, the church and

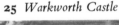

25 *Warkworth Castle*

the market place. Readers of English drama will be interested to note that this is the true setting of the scenes in Warkworth Castle in Shakespeare's *Henry IV*. In 1400 after the outbreak of a rebellion against Henry IV Warkworth was the home of the Percy family. The centre of the town still shows evidence of medieval garden strips or tofts, so that on the available evidence Warkworth was never as crowded as Old Sarum was. The castle and town guard a strategic bridge; because of the winding of the River Coquet, which reaches the sea at a point very near this on the Northumberland coast, there was both a natural water defence and a distinct limitation to the town's size and it does not seem ever to have been extended. The castle guards the undefended side of the town. The market place was in the broad street leading to the church.

26 *Caernarvon Castle*

Caernarvon Castle (**26**) is one of the great royal castles erected by Edward I and Edward II in the northern part of Wales, the homes of much more powerful magnates than a knight. The city, on this occasion, is of much greater importance than either Sarum or Warkworth and the castle's defences stretch out to join those of the rest of the town. A roughly semicircular shape has been created with the water-line as the diameter line. The moat stood on the north front, barely visible in the photograph, and the fortification, consisting of a *curtain wall* linking fortified towers, opened out towards the town and was forced to adopt an unusual interior shape with two baileys as a result. The geometrical pattern or grid of streets preserves the original outline of the town, and it is possible to trace in Fig. **27** not only the general direction of an old wall but to see where the widening of a modern road on the right-hand side has made a gap in the fortification necessary.

27 *Seventeenth-century Plan of Caernarvon*

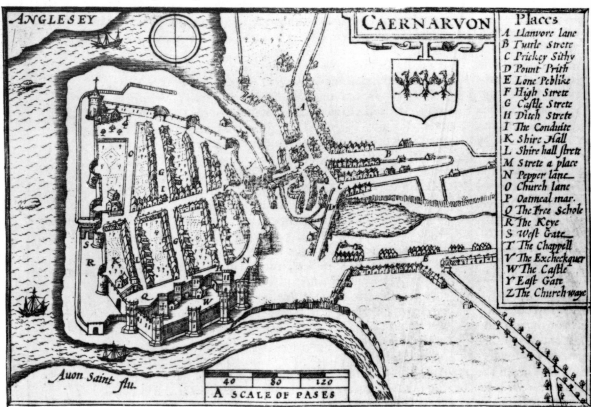

The Knight and his Company

28 *Bodiam Castle*

Our last castle, Bodiam, was built during Chaucer's own times and was one of the most modern of fortifications (**28**). The lake and the stone walls suggest the rustic calm of England rather than warfare, though this, like other castles, was put up on the south coast against possible acts of war from across the Channel. The ground-plan, not shown in the picture, is strictly rectangular with circular towers at each corner, three further towers and a gatehouse also adding to the protection. Even though it was never used as a stronghold it is possible to sense the power and strength of the *machicolations*. The men who built it had the accumulated experiences of centuries of castle building behind them.

After Chaucer's death the need for fortifications declined, until after the accession of the Tudor monarchs they were scarcely necessary. The Elizabethan country-houses which grew out of the abandoned monasteries all over England had little need of fortifications. Only during the Civil War of 1642 did the residents of the castles take their armour down from the walls once more. Thereafter castles relapsed into peaceable sleep.

29 *The Squire*

THE SQUIRE

All readers catch the poet's admiration for the Squire and the unknown illustrator has risen to the occasion well (**29**). With his long sleeves blowing out behind him from his padded *gipoun* or doublet, the Squire has managed to keep on the tall hat under which his crimped hair can be seen. His hose are of a length to put him to extreme disadvantage if he were forced to walk.

It is Chaucer's own notion to place him in the popular context of the activities of the month of May. In his young manhood (a Squire was always under twenty-one) he is a perfect symbol of that time of the human year. In his father's *Tale* the colourless Emelye is addressed similarly:

> Emelye, that fairer was to sene
> Than is the lilie upon his stalke grene,
> And fressher than the May with floures newe—
> For with the rose colour stroof hir hewe,
> I noot which was the finer of hem two.

A garden or a forest in May is the perfect setting for a courtly romance of the Middle Ages, although one cannot forget that in the *Merchant's Tale* there is another character named May, an immoral gold-digger who exploits an aged lover. But in medieval poetry the scene is usually an idyllic one:

> May with alle thy floures and thy grene,
> Welcome be thou, faire fresshe May,
> In hope that I some grene gete may.

The pattern of repetitions there transports the mind at once to the calendar pictures, and, for the best of all, to the *Très Riches Heures*, a most exquisitely illuminated prayer-book owned by the Duc de Berri (who was born in 1340) and executed for him by the brothers Limbourg about the year 1415 (**30**). Note the May Queen on a white horse and in festive attire. She is attended by richly dressed courtiers. The musicians are evidently

30 *The Month of May.*
Pol de Limbourg

31a *and* **31b** *Musicians and their Instruments*

enjoying the occasion and holding their horns up in the manner of a modern jazz trumpeter. This group has gathered the green and made garlands of it. Aries and Gemini are overhead but the lettering of the calendar has been omitted.

Behind the trees is a most carefully executed picture of Riom Castle, one of many owned by the Duc de Berri, with all its slated roofs and turrets. It is a beautiful and formal occasion, presented to the owner of the book to remind him of his own youth, suggestive of refinement and courtesy, catching only a short time after Chaucer's death all that the poet meant to suggest in his references to this month in his poetry.

Since music appears in this episode—the Squire's own instrument was the flute—it may be the moment to consider Chaucer's use of music in *The Canterbury Tales*. The Friar has a harp and a *rote*, which is a three-stringed fiddle. Nicholas the clerk in the *Miller's Tale* possesses a *sautrye* (psaltery), another form of harp, while his associate Absolon plays on a *rubible* (fiddle) and a *gitern*, or guitar. Music evidently excited the medieval mind: at feasts it was essential, and even the Miller had his bagpipe.

The minstrels in these groups taken from MS decorations (**31a** and **31b**) show a typical array of musicianship. The long horns in the first group seem to irritate the other two men. Drums are carried by one man and banged by his partner. Bagpipers, a rote-player and a harpist make up the company.

Vocal music is not neglected in Chaucer's poem. Pardoner and Summoner sing 'Come hider, love, to me'. Nicholas, once more, sings 'Angelus ad Virginem' in a way that suggests a parody of the angel's visitation to the Virgin. In the *Prioress's Tale* the child hero makes much ado about learning the words and music of 'Alma Redemptoris Mater'. In other poems there is birdsong, and group singing both in secular and religious settings.

One of the most beautiful of all the originals in this book is this tournament display shield, that reveals the roles of the knightly lover clad in armour kneeling to his lady, with death awaiting him on the battlefield (**32**). It follows on after the social grace of the courtly scene in Maytime and offers an illustration of the concept of romantic or courtly love, the subject of a great quantity of medieval poetry. As the final ideal of late medieval knighthood it finds its most fitting place in the presentation of the attitudes of the Squire.

An ideal which gave birth to a great corpus of medieval literature is that of romantic love, or *fine amour*. It was an elaborately conceived approach towards personal relations in which the young man gave a reverence to his lady that can best be described as a

32 '*Fine Amour*' (*Romantic Love*)

parody of religion. The youth's position is one of abasement and service: the lady's is one of slowly roused concern or *pitee*. She is beautiful, merciful, tender and compassionate; he is active, ardent and yet diffident.

The golden shield depicts this traditional erotic behaviour with exquisite taste. His facial expression of regretful service and farewell are matched by the seriousness and compassion on the part of the mistress. The expression of the hands is meaningful, and the clothing is as well. He has his visor before him, prior to putting it on and going away to fight. Death, in the shape of a skeleton, as so often depicted, stands behind him. In the lady's shape is moulded all the beauty of the medieval woman who was devoid of rights through her sex but had the power to encourage the deepest courtesy and devotion. Although it is true that much contemporary love-debating was undertaken as a game, there is nothing frivolous in this realization of it. The figures in the Mayday group are perhaps one of the French parliaments of love, meeting to discuss pseudo-questions on that topic, but the characterization of the two young lovers is too intense to overlook or to reject.

Such relationships are examined often in Chaucer's writings. The admiration of Palamoun for Emelye in the *Knight's Tale* (though not that of Arcite for her) is a fine evocation of it. The *Merchant's Tale* enacts a gross parody of it while the *Franklin's Tale* is one of the finest of all its expressions. Searching for lines of Chaucer to offer as a caption for the picture one comes upon this:

> Ther was a knight that loved and dide his payne
> To serve a lady in his beste wise.

The Squire's own tale is unfinished and the one that follows it, the Franklin's, may be read as Chaucer's best revelation of what the Squire left unsaid, as the voice of his age, sex and social station.

THE YEOMAN

It was socially desirable that a Knight and a Squire should have a servant or bodyguard travelling with them. Chaucer was interested in the Yeoman's skill and his appearance, leaving vivid images of both, yet he omitted to provide him with a tale, so that, along with one or two other pilgrims, he is deprived of the right to a narrator's picture in the Ellesmere MS.

The Yeoman is a summery man with a brown face speaking of the outdoor life, but this fine illustration from Pol de Limbourg shows a boar-hunt in midwinter (**33**). The clearing in the trees is in front of the castle at Vincennes where the Duc de Berri himself was born, in December. The power of the picture is in the energy of the animals rather than in the attitude of the human sounding the horn to signify the kill. Both huntsmen carry a boar-spear. One, with his beaver hat, seems of higher rank. The other,

33 *The Month of December: a Boar-hunt.* Pol de Limbourg

who holds the leash of one of the hounds, wears his master's livery-colours at his shoulder. His hose and shoes are in poor state. The hilt of a knife or sword can be seen at his left side.

As a follower of the hunt the Yeoman interests us in what was probably the most popular of medieval sports. Many gentlemen spared no expense in keeping a pack of hounds, taking them all over the countryside and even into church with them. The animals hunted were boar, hare, hart, buck, doe, fox, marten, roe, cat, badger and otter. The boar-hunt here would have been possible in England in medieval times, although it is so no longer. It was the hare that appealed to the Monk and his greyhounds in the next chapter.

Although the Yeoman was undoubtedly representative of the archers who won such a great reputation in battle he is not made a war-like man: in fact, one of the sharpest images in Chaucer's portrait of him is that of the medal of St Christopher on his breast. He allows us to reflect for one moment that the pattern of noble life admitted hunting, which is prominently displayed in the *Knight's Tale* and probably satirized in this extract from the burlesque *Tale of Sir Thopas*, which forms a tailpiece to the section upon chivalry and a satirical comment upon it:

> He koude hunte at wilde deer,
> And ride an hauking for river
>   With grey goshauk on honde;
> Therto he was a good archeer;
> Of wrastling was ther noon his peer,
>   Ther any ram shal stonde.

THE NUNS

The verbal portrait of the Prioress is the most delicately ambiguous of all. In the Elles-mere portrait she is shown in the cloak worn by the Benedictine Order of nuns, with a hood and wimple over her forehead (34). The famous rosary beads are in evidence. Her sister, the Second Nun (35), looks more pensive and is less richly attired. The dress of modern nuns has not altered greatly since the medieval period and this may be the place to remember that the costume of nuns was not entirely distinct from secular female dress during the early part of the fourteenth century when skirts were ankle-length or longer and a wimple was part of the middle-class woman's wardrobe.

34 *The Prioress*

35 *The Second Nun*

The ambiguity in the verbal portrait plays upon the idea of a courtly lady whose attempts to construct a religious life are hindered by her memories of a wealthy back-ground. She cannot refrain from the attempt to re-create it in her cloisters although it is evident to all except herself that the two worlds should remain entirely separate. Nuns were forbidden to wear ornaments, to keep dogs, to expose their foreheads, to travel : in each of these ways she offends. The ironic gestures of praise and blame in the poem are the outcome of the poet's observation of these contrary tendencies in her.

It will be found that the only truly professional item in Chaucer's description is her singing the divine office:

> Ful weel she soong the service divine,
> Entuned in her nose ful semely.

In order to be present on all essential occasions she had a great deal to do. There were seven daily offices starting at 2 a.m. with Matins and Lauds. Then followed Prime, Tierce, Sext, None, Vespers and Compline throughout the day until 7 p.m. in winter and an hour later in summer. The meals at which she shone with her courtly manners were an early breakfast, a midday dinner and a supper between the last two services of the day. It was an arduous routine, if indeed she could carry it all out. Humanity might allow her the consolation of the small dog, for it was traditional that prioresses had one. Just as Chaucer owed some items in the portrait to the *Roman de la Rose*, the most influential of French courtly poems, a reader can also place beside it the more scorching portrait of the nuns of the day from the pen of the Dominican preacher, Bromyard, who speaks of those nuns who: 'provide for their dogs more readily than for the poor, more abundantly and more delicately too; so that, where the poor are so famished that they would greedily devour bran-bread, dogs are squeamish at the sight of wafer-bread and spurn what is offered them, trampling it under their feet.'

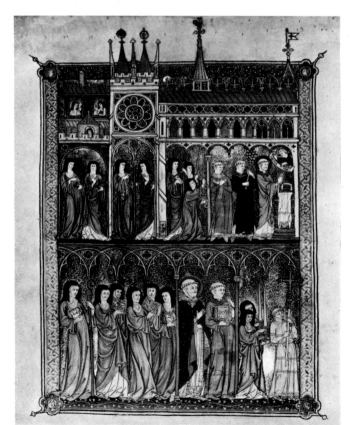

36 *Convent Life*

Knowing that this was a customary attack, one is less inclined to see personal emotion behind the portrait of the Prioress. Once more, Chaucer was capturing in his poetry the most telling and the most popular of attitudes and giving them substance, not aiming to be individual in his judgements.

The crowded plate (**36**) gives both the external shape and the internal life in two scenes shown simultaneously in different parts of a Gothic building. The dress of the nuns is quite attractive and with the music in their hands they are offering a Mass which is being said by three priests—the number of the Prioress's priestly companions. In the group at the bottom of the picture it is probably the nun with the crosier that is the prioress. Note the fine rose-window beneath the twin towers and the three sisters up on the parapet.

This is the first and most attractive of Chaucer's studies of the regular clergy: i.e. those who live together in obedience to a religious rule. It is one of the ironies of the poem that we are only aware of this Prioress because she has broken one of the rules and strayed out on pilgrimage. Her priest, Sir John, is treated separately in Chapter 17 since the interest in his tale is completely different and has little bearing upon his professional tasks.

THE MONK

The ideal of monastic life is not reached by the comfortable man shown in this equestrian picture (**37**); indeed it is emphatically rejected by the presence of two hunting dogs.

37 *The Monk*

38 *The Monk in his Cell*

The work of monks was to offer prayer, practise poverty, chastity and obedience, and devote time to welfare services such as schools and hospitals.

The concept of poverty was ousted when rich people overwhelmed the monks with legacies and benefactions. Where they had done manual work before, they now employed others to do it for them and where they had previously been content with simple quarters, they now extended their buildings and estates until they were well housed in every major town, and owned and farmed great areas of countryside.

Chaucer's Monk, Daun Piers, is only partly to be blamed because he is a victim of the success of his way of life. As 'keeper of the cell' he is obliged to follow the life of a farm bailiff and spend a good deal of time outside the walls of the monastery. Hunting the hare, and his other pastimes, are the sport of the farming community, though by their Rule monks were denied the privilege of hunting, being allowed only to take part in fishing expeditions for the meals of the Friday and Lenten abstinence. The Monk is guilty of being a secularized man seeking the protection of the monastery, a 'manly man', who is to be admired for the undeniable qualities that make him suitable to control the whole monastery but to be criticized for refusing to live by the rule of the monastic Order to which he is sworn.

It is very rare that Chaucer attempts to show the *ideal* type in his collection of portraits. For that let us turn to the beautiful portrait of the Monk in his cell (**38**). The accuracy of the draughtsmanship allows the detail of the robes and the sleeves to be seen. There are manuscripts in his hands and on his shelf, while on the wall is an inkwell. One can also see the illuminated pages of loose manuscripts on which he has been working. This is the ideal of the ascetic life, and is offered also as a portrait of St Jerome, one of the early Fathers.

From the point of view of the student of culture and literacy the copying work of a monk is especially interesting. He represents the period when culture was still largely oral, delivered by word of mouth, and therefore of a completely different nature from that of our own day. It was a time when memory was much more necessary, without written record to refer to; and when recollection of recitations and improvisation on a 'skeleton' story were the common ways in which literary themes were transmitted. For a monk, however, it was different, since he was able to write. Yet, it seems that the very act of reading in the Middle Ages was a noisy one, and a monk in his cell such as we have here would have been heard muttering and forming all his words aloud as if in that way only could he be sure to recollect them. In the *Rule of Saint Benedict* we find this statement, governing just such a scholar as we are discussing: 'After the sixth hour, having left the table let them [the monks] rest on their beds in perfect silence; or if anyone wishes to read by himself, let him read so as not to disturb the others.'

Many of the illuminations in this book come from miniatures at the foot of pages of

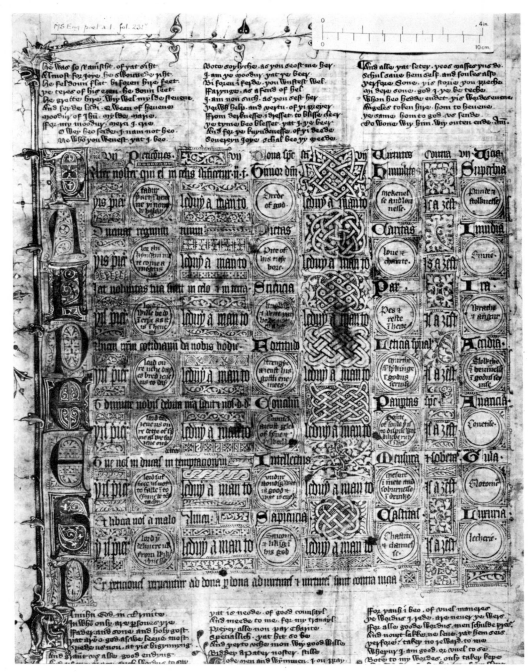

39 *Illuminated MS: the Lord's Prayer*

manuscript. There the imagination of the artist was allowed to develop to the fullest, since the touches of domestic life and outdoor scenery did not need to have any relation to the texts above. In fact, one must not think of a manuscript page as a forerunner of a page of print at all. One is asked to take the page into separate sections, to read along the lines and down the page in the normal way and then to follow the line of the figures up again, turn the page on its side and see what springs to the eye from that angle. Parchment, specially treated sheepskin on which manuscripts were written, was dear, and it was thought a pity to waste any portion of a page. Out of many possible examples two are shown here, one in its entirety and the other without the bottom panel, which appears elsewhere, so that the delicacy and profusion of the well-illuminated page can be seen.

The first is full of script and decorative pattern but crowded with detail (**39**). The reader may be left to interpret it for himself with a number of clues. Down the left margin is a series of illuminated initials which introduce the seven petitions of the Lord's Prayer. The first column of seven roundels provides a Middle English translation of the Latin words. The third column continues the logical structure of a sermon argument that can be based upon each statement. It reads: *leduth a man to* and prints as the next series of religious truths the Gifts of the Holy Ghost, in two languages. The most highly decorated column repeats the words *leduth a man to* and takes the eye along to the series of Virtues, once more in Latin and with a translation in the roundels. The final statement is the series of Sins preluded by the phrase *is agenst*.

This suggests the ground-plan of a series of sermons showing the interrelated thinking which will become quite familiar to the reader of this book. It was evident to the cleric who penned this manuscript that the spiritual life was to be charted as precisely as the sea with its calm spots and its danger zones, and here is one of several such medieval examples set in the middle of a religious poem.

The second example is from the Luttrell Psalter. It is offered as a more disturbing example of the work of medieval artists. The page is beautifully executed (**40**) and one has to turn the page round in order to study the space-filling birds and beasts that have been executed there. The half-human, half-animal figures in the margin, which are to be found in page after page of many versions of the Psalms, have sometimes been interpreted as a series of obsessions. In this respect they may well remind the viewer of some of the startling visions in the pictures of the Flemish artist, Hieronymus Bosch, and, to a lesser extent, in those of Pieter Brueghel. It is more probable that these creatures are examples of sinfulness and evil, intended as didactic examples. Of the lady who is partly a mermaid and partly a bird it is impossible to pronounce judgement, but the man who is partly a lion or similar beast may represent the transforming character of sin which destroys the qualities of the soul and reduces man to the level of the beast. These

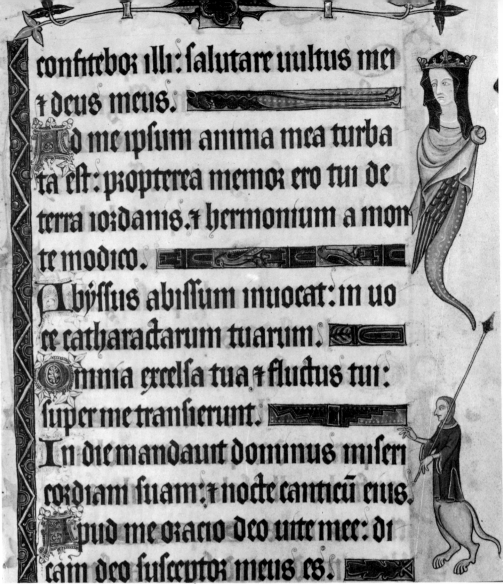

confitebor illi: salutare uultus mei
† deus meus.

Ad me ipsum anima mea turbata est: propterea memor ero tui de terra ioidanis.† hermonium a monte modico.

Abyssus abissum inuocat: in uoce catharactarum tuarum.

Omnia excelsa tua † fluctus tui: super me transierunt.

In die mandauit dominus misericordiam suam: † nocte canticum eius.

Apud me oracio deo uite mee: dicam deo susceptor meus es.

40 *Illuminated MS: a Page from the Luttrell Psalter*

creatures, known as *babewyns*, are sometimes purely comic but more often they have a supernatural power which suggests diabolic possession more strongly than does what we term more comfortably the *Grotesque*. It seems to have been more common in English medieval art than in that of other countries.

In one way, Chaucer's Monk redeems himself when he is called upon to give a tale because he touches upon an important subject—fortune and tragedy—and refuses to provide the hunting story that the Host expects of him. The conception behind his series of short stories may be illustrated by one visual convention of medieval art that has not been touched upon: the Wheel of Fortune.

41 *The 'Queene of Fortune'*

The picture illustrates the 'Queene of Fortune' who presides over a wheel with groups of figures on either side (**41**). They are all learned or courtly people and those who have been flung off the wheel seem not too discomposed by their experience. This is one of many examples drawn from this pictorial convention in medieval art and writing. In simpler pictures it has only four human beings, who embody the rise and fall of princes; and the original Latin names were *Regno*, *Regnabo*, *Regnavi* and *Sum sine Regno* (I reign, I shall reign, I have reigned and I am without a kingdom). From princes and their fall it is a simple transition to other men of power who might ride for a brief time high on Fortune's Wheel—and, incidentally, to the world of Elizabethan tragedy.

Fortune herself was a pagan goddess (Fortuna), but not one of the primary figures such as the Church metamorphosed into the planets. People who were unable to reconcile with religion all the tragedies of life in battle, plague, cold and hunger turned to another deity as a way of explaining what went amiss. She was always termed 'false' or 'fickle', and was often shown as intervening in love and war. Sometimes she was seen figuratively on a mountain or an island. There was always an element of capriciousness in her favours, which the Christian religion did not destroy in the popular mind.

She comes pertinently into this chapter because the *Monk's Tale* is an anthology of stories in which different rulers meet a tragic end. The Monk himself uses the image at the end of one of his narratives:

> Thus kan Fortune hir wheel governe and gye,
> And out of joye bringe men to sorwe.

It is the theme of the entire collection and throws light upon the medieval notion of tragedy:

> Tragedie is to seyn a certeyn storie,
> As olde bookes maken us memorie,
> Of him that stood in greet prosperitee,
> And is yfallen out of heigh degree
> Into miserie, and endeth wrecchedly.

But the accent is not ours. We prefer to blame the State or even the universe for the fall of a good man. In many of the Monk's examples the hero falls from submitting through his own fault to an unworthy passion. Indeed this is how it must be if the place of free will is to be preserved. Man's freedom of choice was stressed even in face of the planetary forces that we shall discuss later: like 'Fortuna', these were the inheritance from pagan religion but still carried weight in the medieval world. Although confronted by all the conflicting elements and zodiacal powers man could, had he the will, evade their grasp; he was not overpoweringly obliged to obey them.

Chaucer discusses the power of Fortune also in the *Knight's Tale*, where the narrative turns upon her cruelties at several points. He cites the subject again in *The Book of the Duchess* and in *Troilus and Criseyde*, and in a small poem devoted to *Fortune*. One of his sources, which he also translated, was *The Consolation of Philosophy* by Boethius. The uncertainty of Fortune becomes one of his favoured formulae; always behind it is the picture of victim on a wheel, and set against it the account of divine love which sought to obliterate from the world the feeling of chaos. It became one of the tasks of the Church to turn this powerful belief in cruel chance to a Christian faith in providential love.

MONASTIC BUILDINGS

It remains to look at architectural settings of the monastic life. Many of our large town churches and cathedrals were monasteries before the Reformation. One of these was Canterbury itself. A photograph may therefore barely distinguish a monastery from other ecclesiastical buildings. Many monasteries, such as Tintern Abbey and Fountains Abbey, are in ruins, while others have been completely destroyed.

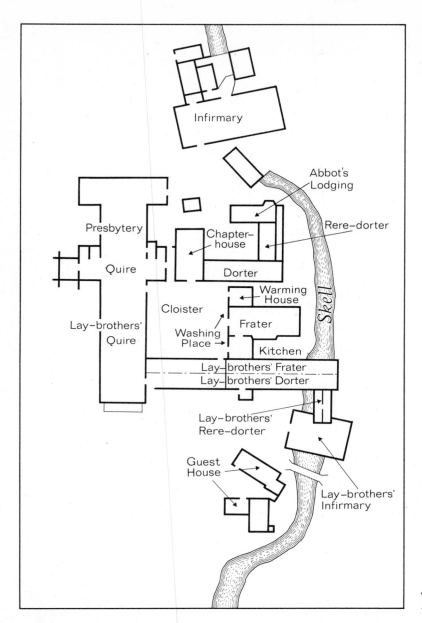

Infirmary

Abbot's
Lodging

Presbytery

Chapter-
house

Rere-dorter

Quire

Dorter

Warming
House

Cloister

Frater

Washing
Place

Lay-brothers'
Quire

Kitchen

Lay-brothers' Frater

Lay-brothers' Dorter

Lay-brothers'
Rere-dorter

Skell

Guest
House

Lay-brothers'
Infirmary

42 *Ground-plan of*
Fountains Abbey

We can learn more about the monastic building by glancing at a ground-plan of a monastery and thinking about the life it had to support. It needed a church as a centre. Since all monks were resident, their living and working quarters could radiate out from the church in a way that no parish church had need to imitate. A refectory, dormitory, infirmary, cellar, wash-house and warming-room were all essential to its domestic economy. The Abbot or Prior would have his own quarters. In the case of the Benedictine Order, whose buildings we shall first be considering, he was likely to be near the

43 *Fountains Abbey*

outside world. Similarly, a guest-house was a normal addition to a monastery; from it the brothers could either earn money as hoteliers or lose it through the unwillingness of their guests to contribute towards their own upkeep.

We can see how the life of the Benedictine monastery fits this pattern. The altar, within the church, was the focus of the way of life; and covered ways, cloisters, leading towards the church, came from the other essential centres. Thus, the monks slept in the *dorter*, which was not far from the church, so that devotions both early and late were quickly accessible. Along the south walk of the cloister might be found the *refectory*, so that kitchens and storage-houses stood as far from the high altar as possible. Further storage-space and cellarage, together with the guest-house, would probably be located along the western walls. The northern walk was the space for study activities and for recreation, being within the sunniest area of the monastery.

Within the precincts there would be the stream which served the function of drainage for the *rere-dorters* or sanitary blocks. There would also be the cemetery, the fishpond and, farther off, the grange, barns and farms. All these were tended by members of the community, so that the monastery became a court, a castle and cathedral all in one when it was fully developed.

Fountains Abbey in Yorkshire, to which we now turn, is an example of the Cistercian abbey with a large number of lay-brothers as well as those who had taken full vows. This division of the monastery led to a duplication of many of the domestic amenities. There was also a far greater tendency in this Order to restrict the use of such communal centres as the chapter-house, and force more seclusion upon the members of the community. Here it will be seen that the Abbot preferred to be in the heart of his small world and not left on the outside to face the distractions there. In the plan (**42**) it should be noted that the *dorter* and the *frater* (refectory or dining-hall) are situated on the floor above the rest of the plan. It has not been possible to identify the site of the cellar, but all the other elements of the monastic setting survive in this ruined twelfth-century abbey (**43**), which is a highly attractive site to visit as well as the largest in England.

Monasteries in towns admitted congregations into their churches, although there was usually a sharp distinction drawn between the areas occupied by the brothers and the lay members of the congregation. When it came to the sudden destruction of monastic buildings at the time of the Reformation, there was hope for the preservation of the main nave of the church if the congregation had become accustomed to worshipping there. Thus it sometimes happens that the monastic church remains while all the other elements are found only in the barest outline in small heaps of stone. Cistercian country abbeys, which had remained isolated and aloof from the general body of the community, were more likely to be completely demolished and left as useless reminders of a way of life deliberately destroyed.

44 *New College, Oxford*

In the universities of Oxford and Cambridge, however, the monastic communities were allowed to survive as colleges. In these the visitor immediately sees such elements of the monastic life as the cloister, the chapel, the library and the exclusively male and clerical body of residents. The appropriate place for a photograph of an Oxford college would be in Chapter 8, but the affiliation of university education with the Church ought to be described here.

New College, Oxford, was founded by William of Wykeham, who was both Bishop and Lord Chancellor, in 1379, when he also founded Winchester School as a source of supply for his Oxford scholars. He intended to provide room for a warden, 3 lay clerks, 10 priests, 16 choristers and 70 scholars who were to be sixteen years of age at their admission to the University.

The cloisters of New College, Oxford, with the chapel in the background offer a number of resemblances to the architectural pattern of monastic life as we have already seen it (**44**). In the foreground is the lawn or cloister garth (one entrance to it is near the right-hand edge of the picture). All round, in the manner of church windows, is the series of lights that flanks the cloister walk. The rough-cast tower, with its stronger edging stones and its octagonal belfry look-out and battlements, was designed to house the college treasures. The papers, moneys, seal, jewellery and ornaments were safeguarded in this Muniment Tower on the principle that the most valuable items were nearest the top. Note, finally, the series of grotesques and the octagonal tower with the slit-windows on the College Chapel.

Readers are invited to compare this scene with Fig. **125** on p. 165 which shows the medieval Old Court of Corpus Christi College, Cambridge. Here the college has no chapel at all (it was built with the near-by St Bene't's Church in mind as an adjunct) so that cloisters are unnecessary. The building on the right is the College Hall, a development from the monastic *frater*. Note the strength of the buttresses, the attic rooms for undergraduates and the cobblestone paths which were formerly to be found in all towns.

In the present age, when university expansion has reached an unprecedented rate, there is an unending debate upon the nature of academic curricula. The newer foundations have widened the scope of their studies while accusing the older ones of remaining in the monastic mode of the Middle Ages. Since the medieval system suggests solitary study and allowance for what we now call research, some authorities have seen going back to contemplative and monastic facilities as the only way forward for an educational system. For this reason the idea of a college has been brought into close conjunction with the idea of a monastery in the present book.

THE FRIAR

The Friar stands third among the regular clergy and ascetics in Chaucer's list. He falls into the lowest place because he is of subordinate rank in his own community, where the other two are of high status. Known to Chaucer and widely spread in England were four different Orders of friars: Dominicans, Franciscans, Carmelites and Austin Friars. Their task was to preach and beg, but they soon became a great deal more prominent:

> As thikke as motes in the sonne-beem,
> Blessinge halles, chambres, kichenes, boures,
> Citees, burghes, castels, hye toures,
> Thropes,[1] bernes,[2] shipnes,[3] dayeryes . . .

[1] villages.   [2] barns.   [3] cattle sheds.

The words from the *Wife of Bath's Tale* suggest the intrusiveness of the friars, which was so widely detested.

The Ellesmere picture shows a dramatic character (**45**). His staff is a reminder of his duty to wander through the countryside as a mendicant, though for the pilgrimage he has been provided with a horse. One can see evidence of socks and of a lining inside his habit in spite of the rule of the Order which stated that 'mantles must be of vile and coarse cloth' and should be felt as a torment and scourge to the flesh.

45 *The Friar*

Although there is a massive literature attacking the friars they were skilled orators, lecturers and preachers, and their university work was without equal. The words of St Francis of Assisi recall readers to a humility and a rejection of the world in the face of a spiritual goal that allows of no possible dereliction or spiritual sloth within the confines of the true fold. A few quotations from St Francis's mandate provide the best commentary on the Friar named Huberd. The Saint advised his followers to 'go and sell all their goods and themselves try to distribute the proceeds to the poor. And the brethren shall see to it that they do not meddle with nor busy themselves with their temporal good nor with the procuring thereof, in order instead they may freely do whatsoever God suggests or inspires in their minds.' St Francis continued: 'I command steadfastly and strictly all the brethren that in no wise they receive any sort of coin or money, either directly in person or through any sort of intermediary.'

It is the history of religious Orders inevitably to abandon such prescripts. In turn new Orders were founded with stricter aims which lasted until it can only have seemed that

46 *Preaching*

asceticism was of very limited appeal. It should, by its demands, make men 'like pilgrims and strangers in this world, in poverty and meekness serving Almighty God' because of the vanity of earthly pleasures:

> This world nis but a thurghfare ful of wo,
> And we been pilgrimes passinge to and fro.
> Death is an ende of every worldly soore. (*The Knight's Tale*)

Contemplation and prayer, spiritual and welfare work were the only courses open to those who accepted the doctrine.

The final picture in this chapter shows a sermon in progress outside a church (**46**). The enthralled audience pays tribute to the friar's energy, even a lame man is making his way into the picture. The effect is one of perfect communication between the preacher and his congregation. Yet since it takes place outside a church it must be assumed that the preacher is at variance with the secular clergy and forced to find his congregation outside—as indeed often occurred. Compare this friar with the picture of the monk in his cell. These are images of medieval religion, which, unlike Chaucer's words, show some of the finer possibilities of medieval asceticism. It was an ideal that was realized more often than it is possible to tell, simply because the ascetic life draws no attention to itself and went unnoticed while it fulfilled its appointed task.

THE MERCHANT

Dealers in every type of produce, and financiers, were familiar to Chaucer, who was born the son of a London wine-merchant. The solemn and outwardly respectable Merchant is linked, as the map (**3**) has shown, with the trade between Suffolk and the Low Countries, while in his spare time he dabbles in possibly illicit foreign currency transactions and lending money at high interest. In the Ellesmere portrait he seems young and stylish (**47**).

47 *The Merchant*

There were probably many rich men at whom Chaucer's word-portrait might have been directed, with its exposure of the sham in the world of impersonal high finance. In Suffolk, the merchants grew rich from the cloth trade and left as memorials the large churches which still surprise the visitor with their height and nobility. The Spring family in Lavenham left such memorials, and so did the Cloptons and others in Long Melford a few miles away. It is possible, however, to identify the Chaucerian Merchant more closely.

A member of the Gild of Merchant Venturers named Gilbert Maghfield was certainly known to Chaucer. He dealt in a variety of wares ranging from hats to millstones, and as part of his livery wore a beaver hat himself. His Gild set up an outpost at Middelburgh and he was known to have introduced safety patrols on the Channel crossing which correspond closely to the Merchant's wish:

> He wolde the see were kept for any thing
> Bitwixe Middelburgh and Orewelle.

More compelling evidence of identification comes from his account-books where he is seen to have recorded loans of money to Geoffrey Chaucer and to his friend, John Gower, also a poet. The illustration (**48**) shows an entry (in French) from his Day Book to the effect that Geoffrey Chaucer owes 28*s*. 6*d*. from 26 July until the following Saturday; it records a loan from Maghfield to the poet to tide him over the end of the month.

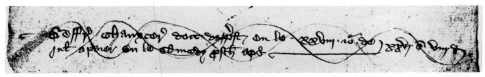

48 *Entry in Gilbert Maghfield's Day Book: 'Geoffrey Chaucer owes 28s. 6d. from 26 July until the following Saturday'*

Maghfield had a large house in Billingsgate of which there is no record. Another merchant of the fourteenth century, named William Haningtone, had a house built with the following specifications: 'A hall and a room with a chimney, and one larder between the said hall and room; one solar[1] over the room and larder; also one oriole[2] at one end of the hall, beyond the high bench, and one step with an oriole from the ground to the door of the hall aforesaid, outside the hall; and two enclosures as cellars, opposite each other, beneath the hall; and one enclosure for a sewer, with two pipes leading to the said sewer; and one stable . . . between the hall and the old kitchen.'

London, in Chaucer's times, was full of such houses. It was still a city in which there was room to move about, with grass, trees and the river visible on all sides. Its sky-line was of great interest because it was common for houses to jut over the pathways, their upper storeys larger than their lower.

It appeared to artists as a pleasant, white, clean, new and romantic place. The fifteenth-century artist who created this picture of the Duke of Orleans confined in the Tower of London may have romanticized, but he left a charming record (**49**). At the right hand the French Duke, in his ermine cape and guarded by armed men, is seen writing a letter. By a device of simultaneous depiction he is also leaning out of the white turret and

[1] Upper room.   [2] Recess.

49 *London from the Tower*

standing outside the door secretly handing his letter to a messenger who will immediately follow the other horsemen leaving the Tower. At the top of the picture the eye makes out London Bridge, the only one across the Thames and in those days fully built upon, and among several church steeples it is presumably Old St Paul's that is visible in the top left-hand corner. It is one of the best pictures that remain of a rich merchant city which, with its 35,000 to 40,000 inhabitants, was many times larger than any other city in the country, and its cathedral larger than St Peter's in Rome.

When the Merchant returns to give his Tale, later in the poem, Chaucer reveals him in a fresh light. There is first a tribute to his colleagues in Northern Italy, then a narrative

50 *The Merchant, Januarie, and the Young Wife, May*

of the utmost cynicism which is one of the finest of the *Tales*. The Merchant, Januarie, and the young wife, May, play an unsentimental game of self-interest, involving also the adultery of Damyan, the squire. The words with which the Merchant ends his *Prologue* lead us to a description of his own unhappily married state in the *Tale*. The illustration (**50**), the work of one of two engravers from Westphalia named Israel von Meckenen, is a century later than the *Tale*, yet it still catches the look of ageing lechery on one side, of false simplicity on the other, while the hands are delving into the money-bag. There is in the girl's hair-band, with its fresh tendrils, the suggestion, found also in the poem, of a wintry Januarie with a young and fertile May.

Chaucer's Clerk is representative of the medieval university student, a 'clerk in holy orders' because he had to take minor orders to be eligible to enter. He may also be considered as a product of the earliest grammar schools, who sent their boys at a very early age to the university, so that much of what today is taught in schools was taught in those times at Oxford or Cambridge. Virtually all medieval schools were run by the Church, although a few were run by gilds. The rich employed chaplains as tutors for their boys and kept them at home until they were ready for college and might then still send their former tutors along with them to keep an eye on their charges. It is likely that the Clerk was destined to return to the teaching profession and serve the community in this manner rather than as a priest.

The portrait shows him huddled in his monk-like habit: the illustrator has contrived to compare the skinny horse and the rapt gaze of the intellectual in a slightly satirical sketch (**51**).

51 *The Clerk*

52 *The University Lecture*

THE MEDIEVAL UNIVERSITY

The lecture session in progress (**52**) shows us that a lecture was originally a reading during the course of which the student might copy down the basic text and hear commentaries upon it at the same time. In the group here only one of the audience has a copy—this was normal and it was customary to find one between three as a common ratio of books to readers in this period before the advent of printing. Some inter-preters of this scene claim that it is a medical lecture with appropriate vessels on the shelf above the speaker. It has also been suggested that these are inkwells and vessels of sand for blotting, the whole structure letting down to form a writing-desk.

The series of detailed and labelled pictures that follows shows the general framework of university education in the Middle Ages extremely well. They are all drawn from a Latin work, *Margarita Philosophica*, by G. Reisch and published first in 1508. Although this is more than a century after Chaucer (and the style of clothing has altered accord-ingly) they may all be taken as representative of the courses of study found in the European universities during the Middle Ages.

When the student who is entering at the foot of the Tower (**53a**), is taken to his first lessons on Grammar he is indeed unlocking the door of knowledge. The first years of a university education which led to a B.A. degree covered these subjects: Grammar (including languages); Rhetoric; Logic or Dialectic. This group is known as the *Trivium*.

The next part of university study leading towards the M.A. degree was divided into the following: Music; Arithmetic; Geometry; Astronomy. Students would, in addi-tion to these last four (known as the *Quadrivium*), study Philosophy—natural, moral and metaphysical. Law, medicine, music and theology might also be studied to the level of a Doctor's degree at the end of another three or four years.

What is immediately noticeable is that everybody received a general education and learned the value of general background knowledge, unrelated to training for a job. In our own day, there is a much greater tendency to specialize and to take technological subjects for a first degree.

The series of plates illustrating the different stages of medieval education is extremely attractive because so much care has evidently been taken in compiling them. It is impossible to say exactly how far the pictorial presentation was in itself traditional, and it has been difficult to arrive at an interpretation of some of the figures and the accom-panying script. The commentary below is intended to offer a basic interpretation and translation of the main subject-matter. There can be no doubt that they are most suitable for the present book since they illustrate abstractions by detailed examples and leave the reader to look again at such small details as the stars in the sky or the half-timbered houses.

Grammar (**53a**). Here the muse welcomes a small boy with a tablet on which the letters of the alphabet are written. Note which letters are omitted in the medieval alphabet. On each floor of this tower is a tutorial room with a 'presiding genius' in command. Thus, the lowest rooms are given to Donatus and Priscianus, whose Latin text-books were the standard works used in all schools in the Middle Ages. Note that

53a *Grammar*

a child is leaving the lowest class and 'going up a class (or grade)' to the stage above.

Completely imaginary portraits are common in early printed books like the one from which the illustrations of this section were gathered. 'The authorities' gazing out of the tower rooms are merely faces representative of important people, as there were no reliable portraits much before Chaucer's time. Aristotle (Logic), Cicero (Rhetoric) and Boethius (Arithmetic) are all universal writers with the whole of literary and philosophical knowledge at their disposal but popularly associated with their writings on these particular fields in the Middle Ages. Boethius, especially, was one of Chaucer's most favoured classical writers: a perfect understanding of Chaucer cannot be made without reference to his debt to him. On the floor above there appear Pythagoras (Music), Euclid (Geometry) and Ptolemy (Astronomy). There is an unidentified face on the floor higher, over which Philosophy presides. Seneca, the tutor in Moral Philosophy (the study of human behaviour), is looking away from the unnamed expert in Physical Philosophy (which corresponds to our own Natural Science). On the topmost pinnacle is Peter Lombard who symbolizes Theology and Metaphysics, the sub-

53b *The Institution of Hebrew and Greek*

jects with which the student completes the university curriculum. A man who had ascended the tower, had learned all that a medieval syllabus could offer.

The Institution of Hebrew and Greek (**53b**). This picture must be read from the top down and then from the left rising to the right. God the Father is shown delivering the tablets of stone (the Ten Commandments) to Moses. Note that Moses is shown with horns, a pictorial tradition that arose from a misunderstanding and which was often repeated. The Michelangelo sculpture of Moses, often considered the finest statue of its day, has the same feature. At the foot of Mount Sinai a group of strongly character-ized Jews are listening to an interpreter who is presumably Aaron. These are repre-sentative of the institution of Hebrew.

The central group is dominated by Cadmus who taught the Greeks their language, according to legend, and came from Palestine to Thebes for the purpose. The third group shows the Latin alphabet once more, as presented by Nicostratus. This completes the languages of antiquity known in the Middle Ages. All the people are dressed alike and in the style of the early sixteenth century, and the artist has given an excellent effect of rocky country that may perhaps be symbolic of the difficult nature of learning.

53c *Rhetoric*

Rhetoric (**53c**). Again a most attractive picture dominated by Seneca and Aristotle (who have both altered facially since their appearance in Fig. **53a**) together with Justinian showing his imperial orb and his legal institutes. The central figure is the muse of Rhetoric whose words create (to the right) the power of the sword and (to the left) the delights and 'flowers' of poetry. For further emphasis she holds a book of history in her left hand and a book of poetry in her right. Poetry is preoccupied with the colours of words, and history with the colours of ideas; the inspiration that the muse gives is sufficient to provide all authorities with the facility to communicate their learning. The hem of the muse's elaborate garment bears the inscription 'the example of meditation' and below it an empty seat labelled 'seat of eloquence', with Cicero and the rhetorician Milo standing near it in the company of a number of unidentified figures.

Medieval rhetoric (discussed in *An Introduction to Chaucer*, Chapter 4) is excellently embodied in this picture. Since it relies entirely upon authorities long dead it is equally applicable to the university curriculum, whether in the age of Chaucer or in the age of Martin Luther.

53d *Logic*

Logic (**53d**). With this the Trivium is complete—the study of languages is an ancillary of the study of grammar and not a separate entity.

The muse is most intricately detailed. In her mouth she has a trumpet which blows out two 'premisses', the major and minor propositions in the logical exercise still known as the 'syllogism', which is the inscription on her sword. Her bow is labelled 'question' while 'argument' is also displayed. At the hem of her skirt appears 'locus' which is probably to be translated as 'passage in an argument'.

The boot that is firmly on the ground is 'fallacy in outside language' and the other (not yet so firmly stamped upon) is 'fallacy within language'. The two little dogs are Truth and Falsehood, the former looking a great deal more happy and prosperous. They are engaged in chasing the hare of Polemics.

The right-hand side of the picture is taken up by the Wood of Opinion, though it may be noted that 'silva' can also be taken as 'the raw material'. Such 'raw material' is provided by the opinions of four thinkers (symbolized by the grove of trees), the four authorities, Albertus Magnus, Thomas Aquinas, Duns Scotus and William of Occam. The undergrowth is labelled as 'insoluble and obligatory', a reference possibly to the unsolved problems of logic.

Finally there appears a dreaming figure, the philosopher Parmenides, whose view was that the earth was a fixed and determined entity and not subject, as his predecessor Heracleitus had maintained, to constant change and flux. He appears to draw his inspiration from the hills which are labelled 'all', 'none', 'a certainty' and 'uncertainty'. On the bottom line appears the legend 'parva logicalia'—the minutiae of logic. With this the concept is completed.

Music (**53e**). An attractive scene with one or two puzzling items. All the performers and the Poet with the crown of laurel represent instrumental and vocal music. Note the finger-technique of the organist. The muse displays the scales which are the basis of all musical notation. It is the figures in the other half of the picture that cause us uncertainties. Tubalcain, the original blacksmith, is shown making what may be part of an instrument, though he may have been introduced on account of the percussive effect of his craft. It seems also possible that there is some confusion here with Jubal, a legendary founder of the art of music. The courtier with the wand is labelled 'pursuivant' and must therefore reflect the ceremonial use of music. The figure in the corner, who could well pass for Shylock, is a problem. Is he weighing elements in an instrument? However, hammers were not used in music-making at that time. He might be displaying the element of balance which, like harmony, is a vital element in a piece of music.

53e *Music*

53f *Arithmetic*

53g *Geometry*

Arithmetic (**53f**). A great deal simpler to interpret. The muse has two open books and a number pattern on her skirt. Boethius is working at arithmetic in more abstract terms although he seems to have a couple of counters on the table. There is a look of complacency on his face which accentuates the unease of Pythagoras still working at his abacus with beads. Note the complex roof.

Geometry (**53g**). This is shown as the basis of surveying and navigation. The pair of dividers, the sextant and the measuring pole are essential in the construction of a barrel or a boat, and the artist has drawn a very fine boat with a single mast, a crow's nest and three banks of oars. The intricate pattern of the individual parts demands a constructional expertise if the safety of the craft is not to be impaired. This is the most practical of the skills that have been displayed in the series of illustrations.

Astronomy (**53h**). Ptolemy being instructed by the muse of Astronomy resembles the earlier sketch of him in the Grammar scene. Although it is presumably daylight the stars are in the sky and he is taking sightings with the sextant from them. At the foot of the picture appears a sketch of the astrolabe, the device with which the position of stars was measured during the Middle Ages. A better picture would show that it was held in the hand (see also the Philosophy scene) and that it was graduated and calibrated so that calculations could be made.

53h *Astronomy*

Chaucer was especially interested in the astrolabe and wrote a treatise upon it dedicated to 'Lyte Lowys my sone' which is accepted as the oldest work in English upon the operation of a scientific instrument. Chaucer opens the First Part thus: 'Thyn Astrolabie hath a ring to putten on the thombe of thi right hand in taking the height of thinges. And tak kep, for from henes forthward I wol clepen the heighte of any thing that is taken by the rewle [the altitude], withoute moo wordes.'

This treatise is evidence of a consuming interest in science which readers of Chaucer will recognize as the source of such well-known astronomical passages as occur in the *Franklin's Tale* and elsewhere. In general, however, the study of the stars is subsidiary to the problems of medicine and a great deal more on this subject will appear in Chapter 12.

Philosophy (**53i**). The summit of human endeavour is the mastery of philosophy. The final scene in this sequence forms the title-page of the book from which it is taken, the beginning and end of all. At the top of the page appear St Antony, the celebrated Bishop of Padua, St Gregory, the great Pope, St Jerome, one of the early Fathers of the Church, and St Ambrose. The emblem in the centre of the group is of the Holy Ghost descending upon man in the form of the dove.

53i *Philosophy*

The three-faced and crowned female figure represents Philosophy with her subsections Natural, Rational and Moral, the regulators of mankind. Once more the seven liberal arts appear, each with her characteristic device. Note the astrolabe in use and the rather comic and vacuous expressions on the sisters' faces. Yet again Aristotle and Seneca the ultimate authorities are reading aloud from their works of Natural and Moral Philosophy.

The question of charges for university education always arises. In the year 1374 it is known that board in an Oxford college cost two shillings a week, and that a student whose bills have been preserved spent £2 a year on his clothes while his tuition fees, rather less, came to 26s. 8d. The collection of twenty books that Chaucer's Clerk assembled may have cost as much as £40. If the student had a taste for the gay life (as had Nicholas in the *Miller's Tale*, who specialized in astronomy) he might not choose to buy so many books. In the Middle Ages, education, like hospital treatment and other welfare services, was the sphere of the Church and the State would never have considered embarking upon such provisions as our university grants.

The final picture shows a medieval bookseller, or possibly his wife (**54**). The thread-bare fellow at the door is an obvious example of the perpetual student like the Clerk himself. The books are recognizably the type that the Clerk has in the pilgrim portrait. Since a stock of them is being offered for sale it means that towards the end of the period of script stocks of popular books are kept in a number of shops.

In the end we accept the Clerk but do not find him especially attractive to us. When asked to begin his *Tale* he offers a lesson in Italian geography which once more embodies the poet's irony towards some of the sterilities of academic education. He preferred, it must be admitted, the Monk who is at least a 'manly man' where the Clerk is unworldly and reserved.

54 *A Medieval Bookseller*

THE SERGEANT OF THE LAW

An analogy with the military rank of sergeant must not blind us to the fact that a Sergeant of the Law was formerly a very important barrister, having practised with distinction for at least sixteen years before he was eligible for the position. The poet's words give assurance of detailed knowledge. The Ellesmere picture shows the lined cape and hood associated with his rank. A special significance resides in the 'robes' which he would have been wearing underneath his outdoor habit (**55**). In order to win them he had served a magnate desiring to extend his lands and needing an official hand to steer him through the maze of complexities that beset the purchaser of land in those

55 *The Sergeant of the Law*

days. The retaining fees and the livery robes were a sign of his dependence upon a noble household and may hint at sharp practice in obtaining the rights to some parcels of land. If everything to him was 'fee simple' it suggests that he had no trouble in establishing his lord's claim to property; but it may also suggest some underhand activities that went on in the territorial aggrandizement of a land-hungry noble who had the law on his side when he had fed his competent Sergeant well.

56 *The King's Bench Court in the Fifteenth Century*

In the scene depicting the King's Bench Court in the fifteenth century there are chained prisoners at the foot of the picture and one miserably at the bar, while five judges are hearing the cases (**56**). The lined tunic, the hood and gown are the robes of the medieval judge, the gown being known as an *armelausa*. Instead of a modern wig the headgear is a *coif* which is also worn by the counsel standing beside the prisoner. Note the long scrolls on which all official records were kept and the parti-coloured robes

57 *The Chancery Court in the Fifteenth Century*

which were often predominantly green or brown. These are the robes for which the Sergeant worked so hard.

In the Chancery Court scene (**57**) the judge is the Lord Chancellor, the head of the legal profession. Beside him sits the Master of the Rolls. Note that all except the Chancellor are tonsured. There are no defendants in this court, only a succession of clerks and the well-robed sergeants as before.

58 *The Franklin*

THE FRANKLIN

Chaucer makes the Franklin the travelling-companion of the Sergeant so that one scents a professional association between the lawyer and the rich landowner who is apparently more at home in the country than the Knight, his social superior. Though his social position is less significant we sense that he knows how to live like a lord and devotes a great deal of time to eating and drinking. The Ellesmere portrait shows an old man of florid temperament with the *gipser* on a cord at his side as the text prescribes (**58**).

This man's place in the *General Prologue* is as a sanguine figure of festivity and plenty. Reading the poem that describes him it is significant to recall this statement from a writer on the history of feasting: 'Our ancestors ate practically everything that had wings, from a bustard to a sparrow, and everything that swam, from a porpoise to a minnow; but in the matter of fruits and vegetables they came off very badly.' It was customary at that time to take two main meals: a dinner in mid-morning and a supper fairly early in the evening. The Franklin added to this his 'sop in wine', a concoction of wine, almond milk, saffron, ginger, sugar, cinnamon, cloves and mace, all poured over the best quality bread.

As a reminder of the spiritual dangers of such self-indulgence here is the moralist's picture of the last drink after supper (**59**). Music is being played. The food has been cleared away and only the drink remains. Note that only the host has a seat, an indication of the scarcity of furniture in all households. A disgruntled cleric is begging at the side. He is out of luck and in the right-hand panel the artist appears to have projected his dark thoughts. Three figures from the group of drinkers reappear in the infernal depths. This is a further comment upon the sin of gluttony and a complement to the observations in the next chapter on the Cook.

The Franklin, teller of the *Tale*, seems to be largely distinct from this man. His *Tale* has already been mentioned as a fine realization of the ideal of romantic love and does not warrant further discussion here, except to point out that this is one of the poet's most sensitive and distinguished narratives.

59 *The Dangers of Self-indulgence*

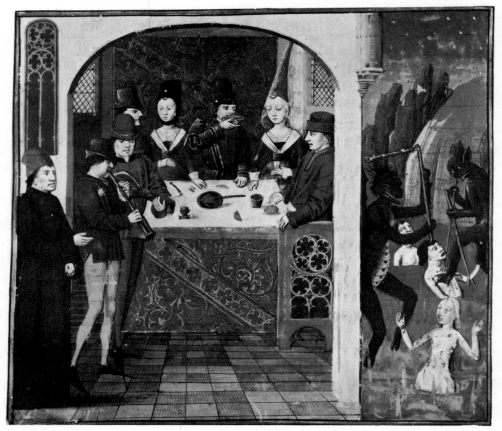

THE MANCIPLE

Although we have taken the Manciple out of sequence to include him at this point there is no harm in so doing. Chaucer himself was apparently very little interested in

60 *The Manciple*

him, and filled up the portrait confusingly with portraits of the young men he served in one of the Inns of Court where he was in charge of the domestic arrangements. The Ellesmere portrait supplies inexplicable flasks which add nothing to his characterization (**60**).

The building is the Old Hall (and, at the left side, the Chapel) of Lincoln's Inn, London (**61**). From the thirteenth century the Inns of Court had operated as legal colleges attached to the Law Courts. They are best appreciated as post-graduate foundations intended for landowners and professional men who, in the first instance, had usually been educated at Oxford or Cambridge. The organization of the Inns resembled the universities for this reason. Staircase 17 has the names of occupants of chambers in precisely the way that the names of undergraduates and senior members are displayed in the older universities. The Hall in universities is more used for dining than for any academic purpose. In Lincoln's Inn there was a Hall in the thirteenth century that was standing in Chaucer's day, but the present building dates from the end of the fifteenth century and is the oldest extant part. The two bay-windows and the parapet will be familiar from the other architectural studies in this book. Note the octagonal lantern

61 *The Hall, Lincoln's Inn*

on the roof. The neighbouring Chapel dates from the reign of James I but it retains the older form of rose-window with Perpendicular traceries.

The interest in the Manciple's portrait shifts from the man to the students who were living under his care and from them to their future employers. Throughout the verse-paragraph the poet's attention wandered, but it has a centre in the financial methods of this insignificant Manciple, relating him to the Sergeant of the Law whose financial acumen is also singled out by Chaucer. The Manciple, however, is shown as an illiterate man serving highly literate masters. His method of handling debits and credits bears no relation to careful book-keeping. He uses the notched tally stick (*taille*) that was a standard record of a debt at a time when it was not possible for every transaction to be recorded in writing or every payment to be made in silver bullion because of the sheer weight of it. In effect a tally, a piece of hazelwood about nine inches in length, was a lasting record of a bill and a cheque as well. It came to be the practice to hand them on to third parties who would accept them much as small shops will take our third-party cheques nowadays.

These were not only used for personal debts: the Exchequer dealt in them. From the year 1414 there is a note preserved saying that Thomas Chaucer, the poet's son, complained of a long overdue debt for official purchase of wine amounting to hundreds of pounds, and nobody was willing to meet the tally.

62 *The* Taille, *or Tally Stick*

It will be noticed that the tally (**62**) has six deep notches representing pounds, thirteen more on the underside to record the shillings and eight penny cuts to complete the statement. There would have been seals affixed but these are no longer visible.

The majesty of the law was associated in Chaucer's mind, it seems, not so much with the delays as with the marginal profiteering that accompanies it. From the lowest rung of the ladder, the Manciple and all his legal students, to the top, the Sergeant, he outlines for his readers a profession geared only to selling its services at the highest and most cunning level of extortion. Throughout the ages this view has been shared by victims of its delays and exorbitances.

Chaucer's intentions towards the members of the parish gild, away on their pilgrimage, were generally mischievous. He was more concerned with ill-judged aspirations towards civic pride and power than with their technological proficiency. He allows them no individual life and no tales; he even refuses to make them members of the larger trade gilds, and so they are all heaped together in a single gild that had to legislate for several trades and bring everybody together for social and religious activities.

It will be noticed that four of the five gildsmen—Weaver, Dyer, Tapicer and Haberdasher—are connected in a humbler way with the cloth trade. There are no members of the food trades, a fact which makes the Cook a welcome extra.

63 *The Warden of a Gild
with two Craftsmen*

In the illustration (**63**) the warden of a gild sits in judgement on the work of two young craftsmen, a stonemason and a carpenter, who represent all the building trades and appear to be apprentices applying for full admission. The ermine-robed warden has an eye for technical proficiency while the poet has pointed out social shortcomings. He picks out the silver knives and leaves the reader with an analysis of local politics—that it was controlled by simpletons with pushing wives who qualified for the honours in civic life by reason of their wealth.

The interior of The Merchant Venturers Guildhall in York is a most impressive one (**64**). It was built in the 1350s and 1360s and is in a fine state of preservation. Acting as the headquarters of a very lively fraternity it had space for a chapel, for large meetings,

64 *The Merchant Venturers Guildhall, York*

65 *The Cook*

and a few residents. It concerned itself with all matters arising from the export of cloth to countries as far afield as Japan and China. On other pages of this book exteriors have been shown, but this photograph shows the great strength and solidity of timber that lies behind the façades of so many medieval buildings. This is typical of medieval castles and halls with its naked beams and the heraldic banners on every post. On the dais are the official weights for the merchandise and at the back, portraits of later masters of the gild. It was the aim of all Chaucer's gildsmen 'to sitten in a yeldehalle on a deis': this is the best possible illustration and example to visit.

In the case of the Cook the poet has devoted some space to his technical prowess. The Ellesmere picture shows the simple costume with the meat-hook serving as an emblem (**65**). The reflections of the writer on the *mormal* or sore on the man's shin have been mirrored by the artist. The highly flavoured goods which are elements of good living are sharply contrasted with the skin eruption, a reminder of bad living.

The seasoning which he underlines as part of the cook's art may have come from a need to hide the rottenness of his ingredients. The Host reveals in the opening to the unfinished *Cook's Tale* that in the cookshops of the period there was a good deal of

66a *and* **66b** *Cooking Operations*

unwholesomeness rampant and 'many a flye loos'. For this reason Chaucer makes the cooks in the *Pardoner's Tale* seem to be so frenzied:

> Thise cookes, how they stampe and streyne and grinde,
> And turnen substaunce into accident.

The illustrations of cookery in action show exactly this (**66a** and **66b**). There is no sign of a great medieval oven here but notice the meat-hook and the man pounding his ingredients in a huge mortar. The rabbit being dismembered seems to be aware of his surprising fate and all the men have the distorted or mannered features found in early medieval Gospel scenes.

In many of his courtly poems Chaucer has an opportunity to describe feasting and the Franklin is a total embodiment of such a life. Chaucer preferred simpler cooking himself, heightened with a little flavour. Beyond that, he says, all is sinful, and pleasing only to the wickedly gluttonous character 'to fulfille al thy likerous talent'.

The Shipman is one of a large number of men who owned small ships of about 200 tons and hired them for mercantile purposes all over Europe. In times of war the small ships were fortified with the addition of two castles (forecastle and aftercastle) and became warships.

The Shipman (**67**) is shown in his gown of *falding*, a serviceable and not a cheap material, and the 'daggere hanginge on a laas' is a reminder of his tougher nature. An

67 *The Shipman*

illiterate, he was able from experience to find his way round the shores with the maps which were, in any case (like parts of that on p. 101), far from reliable as a practical guide to navigation. But Chaucer does not hide the fact that the Shipman was concerned in two unscrupulous practices typical of sailors of the period.

First, he attacked other vessels and made the men walk the plank. Piracy of this type was feared by every merchant who exported his goods; in this respect the portrait of the Shipman complements that of the Merchant, who was an employer of seamen, and wanted the North Sea kept clear of pirates. The Shipman's thefts of wine were also commonplace in Chaucer's lifetime, and a measure passed to counteract this petty

68 *Ships at Anchor*

pilfering instituted checks upon the contents of standard wine-casks at each end of the
wine's journey from France or Spain to England.

The type of ship called a barge is illustrated here (**68**). There is evidence of castles on
two of these craft. The one at the extreme left has a stern rudder, while the one to the
right of the picture has signs of cargo on board. The ships have a gracefulness and a
rounded quality of moulding that is most pleasing, while the perspective of the whole
scene resembles that of some delicate Oriental landscapes with the dominating ships in a
spatial dimension of their own. Note the public execution in the background.

It has been pointed out that Dartmouth was especially notorious for the brutality
of its sailors. When Chaucer placed the Shipman in that port he was probably inviting a
prepared response from knowledgeable people. The records show how inhospitable
both Devon and Cornwall were to any sailors cast up on shore and how rapacious for
stolen goods the local mariners were. It adds a further point to an already equivocal
portrait. There can be no doubt that the poet intended his readers to criticize the brutality of piratical sailors but that he himself was impressed by the strength, the imposing
bearded appearance and the expert knowledge of the master-mariner.

The map above (**69**) is an artist's impression of Dartmouth in Devon, the home of the
fictional Shipman of Chaucer and of a number of real-life pirates which gave the port a
dangerous reputation. The typical Dartmouth seaman had the same lack of tender
conscience that Chaucer attributes to his seafarer.

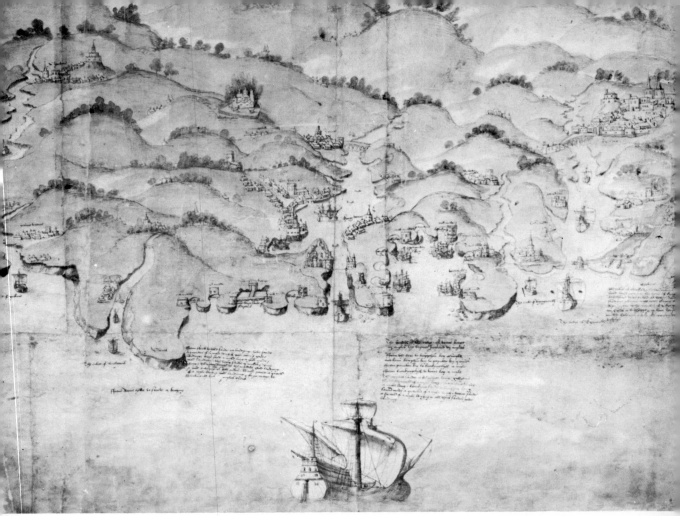

69 *Dartmouth*

It is not an accurate representation of the area. In an age long before the introduction of aerial photography it is difficult to imagine how it can have been compiled. No look-out from the crow's nest of a passing ship can ever have seen so deeply into the heart of the hills and to all the little communities that are seen over a large area. Concentrate upon the general picture it creates of waterway, hill and, above all, of the sea and the magnificent ships which suggest the days of Francis Drake, another great Devonian. The maker of the Gough Map on p. 8 was scrupulous in his treatment of cartographic symbols and of distances. The early Tudor maker of this one was not. Nevertheless he has drawn a map fascinating to study despite its inaccuracies.

The social and intellectual standing of the Doctor is suggested by the taffeta robes, lined with fur, and the phial of medicine carried as a symbol even though he is riding on horseback (**70**). To have graduated in medicine at a university in the Middle Ages, any student would have been obliged to review a great deal of theoretical learning based on the positions of the planets and on the signs of the zodiac as well as on the nature of the

70 *The Doctor of Physic*

constitution of the body. In France, particularly, it was a rule that doctors could be deprived of their practice if they failed to display an almanac which would tell them the favourable days—in accordance with astrological calculations—for blood-letting and other treatments. There is little doubt that Chaucer's Doctor is a worthy symbol of the medical profession and the description implies a sincere appraisal of his ability.

71 *The Zodiac Man*

CELESTIAL INFLUENCES

It is said, for instance, that the Doctor used 'images' to assist in cures. These were small reproductions of the signs of the zodiac which were to be placed on the seat of suffering at the right time when the sign of the zodiac was at its height. In his illustration the body is shown encircled by all the signs, each of which has a sphere of influence (**71**).

72 *The four Humours*

Thus, for instance, Gemini is represented by a two-headed figure (though in other accounts they are described as two separate ones who stand on either shoulder). The reader is invited to study this chart with care and to compare it with the signs of the zodiac shown in the miniatures on p. 23 (**8**). Naked manikins of this type are found in page after page of medical tracts of the time, all over Europe, so that there was international agreement on the validity of directing the student towards such study in all the universities. Since the present illustration comes from a MS in the Vatican Library it could be said that this is basically a pagan practice which was nevertheless sanctioned by the Church, giving rise to the views of the atheism of doctors expressed in the Chaucerian gibe that the Doctor's study as a medical man was 'but little on the bible'. Even so, there are angels on hand to bless the work.

In the medical literature of the Middle Ages are found illustrations such as the 'Disease Man', the 'Vein Man', the 'Planet Man', and the 'Pregnant Woman', all self-explanatory.

Pagan gods, discredited though they were by Christian thinkers, were never outgrown. At one time they were explained as historical persons. Since many people continued to believe in their limited and non-coercive powers they were admitted to the realm of the planetarium from which they could look down upon earth and mankind as spectators, if nothing else. It was not until the coming of the Renaissance that they were explained as the mythological figures we now know them to be, and interpreted as allegories. In Chaucer's time they were thought to affect the growth and development of all created existences and lives.

THE FOUR HUMOURS

What was not thought to have been determined by celestial influences was most probably conditioned by the 'humours' of the body. Today we discuss these effects in the form of genes and glands to similar purpose. The four humours were symbolically associated with deities so that the inner manifestations of one locked a man into the external powers of the other and man might find himself trapped. This order is often found (**72**):

Melancholy	cold and dry humour	Saturn
Choler	hot and dry humour	Mars
Phlegm	cold and moist humour	Moon
Blood	hot and moist humour	Venus

In order to understand this more fully we may turn to the fourteenth-century writer Bartolomaeus Anglicus for a few notes:

Melancholy. This man, under the effects of an excess of his natural humour, is said to 'love and desyre dethe' and to be readily given to both delusions and depression: 'If they here cockes crowe, they rere uppe theyr hondes and armes and smyte themselfe, and syngynge thynke them selfe to be cockes.' In our illustration there is a fine and sensitive sad face (whose early Tudor costume is of a century later than Chaucer's) and whose long hair and sleeves add rather to a sense of dignity than to a sense of madness. He carries in his hand a scroll which says: 'Ther are the four humours'.

Choler. A man affected by this humour soon becomes 'unkyndely' and 'wrathful, hardy and unmeke, lyght, unstable'. They ruin themselves if they eat 'lekes, oynions, garlike and of such kynde'—a resemblance so immediately reminiscent of the Summoner that it cannot be overlooked as a possible origin of that character's excessive humour. In the illustration the dark coloration and beard may well suggest a fiery nature but there is a fineness about the portrait that forbids us to see him as in any way dangerous. In his hand the scroll reads 'Hafyng the [four fingers to stand for the number] kynd of hues'.

Phlegm induced excesses of sloth and its subjects are said to be 'fatte, greate and shorte and croked in extremyties', their skin 'pleyne and smothe without heare'. The figure in the bottom right-hand corner is at least slightly crippled and has a dullness of countenance which confirm the analysis. He also seems to be cold since he alone wears gloves and he has the least attractive appearance of the group. His scroll reads 'They ar reservid un to the four elements'.

Blood being a sign of heat and youth is also a symbol of the healthier aspects of the sensual life. It was recognized that too much 'blood' or passion in an older man can cause him to fall down in what we class as a heart attack. There is again a slightly refined sensuality about the figure of Sanguine. His costume is a sign of nobility and his hat is a fashionable one. His scroll reads 'Thay are o[f] disysse calde the four complecious'. All the words in these scrolls present difficulties to the reader and it may even be the case that although this is an English manuscript the scribe engaged was foreign.

It must not be thought that every movement of the humours in the body was destructive: far from it, for all the excellences of human character spring from the same sources. As the planets changed their positions hour by hour and day by day so did the strength of their influences upon the humours in the body and the entire nature. The doctor's task was to act as an intermediary; a family medical adviser would undoubtedly possess the charts of the lives of all his best patients so that he could apply his remedies at the sanctioned time.

While one remembers that these planetary forces were an inheritance from pagan religion, and that man's basic freedom of choice was always emphasized, one conclusion that is readily drawn from these images and figures is that man could hardly be described as a free agent. He was bound to the earth, and it was as if the different forces played with him for his body and soul. It then follows that God (in the centre of the illustration of the Humours) was perfectly aware of the influences and correlations, and had therefore decided it should be part of the divine purpose of each individual's life. Indeed, if we add together all the possible forces that might be operative man could truly call himself a *microcosm* (a small world) which was both the mirror and the plaything of the *macrocosm* (the whole universe). By describing man as strapped down while greater powers had their way with him, it is easy to understand these two technical terms that are often invoked in the study of medieval and Renaissance thought and often arise in the discussion of the order, disorder and chaos images in the works of the major writers of the period, most especially in the works of Shakespeare.

AILMENTS AND TREATMENTS

For a more detailed investigation of medical concepts as they relate to *The Canterbury Tales* the reader may be assured of a great deal of illumination from W. C. Curry's book

73 *Manipulative Surgery*

a　　　　*b*　　　　*c*

d　　　　*e*　　　　*f*

Chaucer and the Medieval Sciences. But the Chaucerian portrait of the medical practitioner is not without its tribute to his simpler skills. It tells of the money he made, and if it had been longer it might have outlined some of the courses of treatment that followed after the careful nocturnal diagnosis. The miniatures have been chosen from a large number that still survive (**73**). The six scenes depict common troubles and since the patients are so young one might even hazard the guess that they are suffering from dislocations caused during a hearty game of football! With the help of his assistants the patient is being variously manipulated. In (*a*) it is a dislocated shoulder; in (*b*) an elbow; (*c*) and (*d*) are strained wrist and hand, while (*e*) is a different shoulder case. The last (*f*) is a scene in which the patient is being advised about his prescription.

A final touch in Chaucer's comprehensive passage concerns the fees paid during the pestilence. This refers to the attacks of plague that came to England after 1348 and continued until between one-third and one-half of the population had died of it. All occupational groups were depleted and in many cases villages were depopulated and abandoned as a result. An economic effect was the increase of sheep-farming at the expense of arable cultivation and a longer term one was the feeling of dissatisfaction at their treatment registered by the labouring men who had survived, which culminated in the Peasants' Revolt of 1381.

The infinite tragedy of the Black Death is too immense a subject for it to be treated as a medical matter only. The Parson, the Plowman and many other pilgrims could have given their testimony on this tragic event, but it falls into the Doctor's purview, and he 'kepte that he wan in pestilence'. There is no illustration which adequately conveys the effect of the pestilence on those who lost.

The inscription on the wall of Ashwell Church has many tragic aspects (**74**). It is to be found some ten feet from the ground scratched on the wall of the tower at a time when building had been abandoned because of scarcity of labour. There is no way of knowing who it was that left this inscription but it looks back to a whole lifetime of misery. There are barely decipherable letters near the top left-hand corner which tell in Latin 'The first plague was in June 1300'. A little lower but above the main line of writing is 'XLIX pestilencia' a succinct reminder of the Black Death itself. Then occurs a longer message which transcribed reads 'M Ct Xpenta, miseranda, ferox violenta. Superest plebs pessima testis in fineque ventus validus. Oc anno maurus in orbe tonat.' The translation reads: '1350: wretched, wild and driven to violence the people remaining become witness at last of a tempest. On St Maur's day this year 1361 it thunders on the earth.'

This urgent message for posterity is more compelling than a picture of a row of corpses. One final date is also engraved. Beneath the first the date 1649 is decipherable —the year of the execution of Charles I. An Ashwell royalist saw the execution as a

74 *The Black Death leaves its Mark*

similar tragedy and as the end of an era in exactly the same way. Glancing at this inscription with a mind sympathetically open to an experience that none of us can ever expect to comprehend we have some idea of what is meant in the second half of the fourteenth century by the words 'deeth' and 'pestilence'.

The Wife of Bath, so much her own mistress, so often a wife, is a figure of shameless vitality (**75**). Chaucer's portrait is a perfect enactment of character through breathless monologue. Illustration is barely necessary but note the foot-mantle, the large hat, the whip which symbolizes domination and the wimple which was already out of date as a middle-class lady's choice at the time Chaucer was writing. The wife rides astride, like a man, and wears spurs.

75 *The Wife of Bath*

The *misericord* (the small rail underneath a choir-stall) shows a husband being beaten by a shrewish wife (**76**). She is caught in action, pulling his beard and lashing out with a shovel. Alisoun the wife hit out until her most recent husband renounced his natural domination and handed over to her the sovereignty she always desired.

76 *The Wife beating her Husband (Misericord in Carlisle Cathedral)*

From the viewpoint of medieval physiognomy, no single planet could explain this feminine whirlwind. The influence of the goddess Venus was only a small part of her planetary inheritance. It is typical of the Venusians that they should be sexually attractive, and the Prioress has this quality with her broad forehead and her red lips. In the German illustration (**77**), taken from the *Mittelalterliche Hausbuch*, Venus hovers overhead on horseback between Libra, the scales and Taurus, the bull. There is music from fife and tabor and dancing by 'tumblers' and a little sexual exploration on the right of the group. A group of more courtly dancers, dressed in the costume of the May revellers, appears lower down, while a bath-house attendant is ministering to the food and drink requirements of two lovers intent on sharing a bath (a common German custom).

According to medieval ideas of planetary influence Venus had an influence over her children of a kind which led them to adopt certain activities or professions; the fourteenth-century encyclopaedist wrote that Venus 'disposeth to fayrenes, volupte[1] and lyking,[2] in touche and groping, in smel and taast, and in songe. And therefore he maketh singers, lovers of musike and makers of confection of spicery and spicers. Under

[1] lustfulness. [2] appetite.

77 *Venus and her Children*

78 *Mars and his Children*

hym [i.e. the planet] is conteyned love, frendshyppe and pylgremages; and tokeneth winninge, ioye and blysse.' (Note the group of card-players, symbolizing 'winninge'.)

Chaucer describes the further ramifications of the worship of Venus in the *Knight's Tale* when Palamoun visits her temple. Around its walls are found scenes very like the illustration given here, composed of several related panels or incidents:

> Festes, instrumentz, caroles, daunces,
> Lust and array, and alle the circumstaunces
> Of love, which that I rekned and rekne shal,
> By ordre weren peynted on the wal,
> And mo than I kan make mencioun.

Dancing, a symbol of 'love, the olde daunce' appears often in medieval poetry as a symbol of courtship and union. It is featured among the visions conjured by the clerk in the *Franklin's Tale*. The knight in the *Wife of Bath's Tale* sees another group of dancers who disappeared:

> Vannished was this daunce, he niste where.

Absolom in the *Miller's Tale* and Perkin in the *Cook's Tale* are two other dancers.

The influence of Mars, on the other hand, was more baleful. Bartolomaeus wrote that Mars 'dysposeth the soul to unstedfaste sytte and lyghtnes, to wrathe, and to boldnes, and to other Coleryke passions. Under him is conteined warre, bataile, prisonne and enmyte. And he tokeneth wrathe, swyftenes, and woundes, and is redde and untrue and gylefulle.' The illustration shows how Mars urges his children to follow him (**78**). Robbery, violence and destruction are found seizing upon a village. At the foot of the picture there are more personal and no less horrible manifestations of the cult of violence. Note, too, the pugnacious wife laying about her with a large jug and another with a distaff; two German Alisouns in peasant costume.

In the *Knight's Tale* the Martian is Arcite, the more virile of the two young men. His visit to the temple underlines all the familiar qualities:

> The statue of Mars upon a carte stood
> Armed, and looked grim as he were wood;
> And over his heed ther shinen two figures
> Of sterres, that been cleped in scriptures,
> That oon Puella, that oother Rubeus—
> This god of armes was arrayed thus.
> A wolf ther stood biforn him at his feet
> With eyen rede, and of a man he eet;

This is from a different tradition of Martian iconography but the emotion is unmistakable.

The Wife of Bath, then, is an amalgam of these two planets. To Mars she owes her pugnacity of disposition, while it is to Venus that she owes her flaunting sexiness and the genuinely attractive aspects of her nature. She is a useful lesson in medieval character-analysis and astrological study who says of herself:

> I am al Venerien
> In feelinge, and myn herte is Marcien.

Nobody would dispute the Wife's supremacy in the field of sensuality. We leave her, then, in the context of the Wheel of the Senses (**79**) from the wall of Longthorpe Tower, near Peterborough, where it was painted along with many other allegorical pictures during Chaucer's lifetime. Note the large royal figure of Human Reason transcending the animals perched on the five-spoked wheel. The monkey symbolizes Taste; the vulture symbolizes Smell, which leads her to her prey. The spider's web is a delicate tracery to the Touch; the boar's keen Hearing and the cock's Sight, enabling it to see the rising Sun, complete the group, and remind us that in these ways animals surpass human beings, who have reason and the soul as their guiding principle. The original is in an imperfect state today: a drawing of it is shown in its place.

79 *The Wheel of the Senses*

THE PARSON AND THE PARISH CHURCH

The Ellesmere Parson rides in a simple clerical habit, his hands crossed on his breast in a gesture of piety and submission. This expresses his ideal professional work as preacher, confessor and Mass-sayer (**80**).

80 *The Parson*

A medieval parish church illuminates his task and symbolizes it. Hanwell Church in Oxfordshire is depicted here as a comparatively clumsy example of the parish church, at the farthest extreme from the cathedral style of decoration, typical of the village church in England (**81**). An immediate glance shows that it grew slowly. In this case, note that at a point about half-way down the *nave* the design changes completely as a new *chancel* was added to the existing one. At the same time or later a wing or *aisle* with a large porch was also added. This has caused some blocking of the windows high up in the *clerestory*, for they are only partly visible.

81 *A Medieval Parish Church (Hanwell, Oxfordshire)*

The windows on the west end, especially the one in the centre of the photograph, are examples of *lancet windows* with diamond panes, while the one beside the porch is of even greater interest. It has the same overall arch-shape as the porch, and is composed of three lancets whose *mullions* curve gently over at the top and form three larger diamonds under the main arch.

The tower is battlemented, although comparison with the battlements of a castle shows that those of the church are lacking in defensive strength. The spiral stairway up to the roof and the bell-chamber aloft has *slit-windows* without glass. An unusual feature is a triangular *buttress* forced in between the roof of the south aisle and the tower, in order to prop it up. An inch or two above its meeting-point with the tower note a small piece of what seems to be the original roof-line.

There is little evidence of external decoration apart from a single feature over the south aisle in the centre of the photograph. In general the church lacks individuality, but has instead that suggestion of restfulness and nostalgia which is always associated with a weathered country church building.

Inside all parish churches there were many surfaces for decorative schemes. A building that may have been dark (since candles were allowed on the altar alone) and without any pews at all during the fourteenth century had as compensation a great deal of imagery painted and carved over it. For traces of it the viewer can look at every point of intersection along constructional lines inside the church and out and at the crosses, lecterns and tombs that are scattered around the interior. Subsidiary chapels dedicated to rich families often yield much artistic material, as do the decorated benches, the capitals at the tops of pillars and the pulpit. Although they have now almost disappeared there is no doubt that wall-paintings once abounded in churches. These have perhaps been weathered away or hidden in whitewash, but there is much evidence to show that the church was the most colourful building that many country people knew.

CHURCH IMAGERY

One special image found in English churches was a large picture of St Christopher, the Christ-carrier. There was a superstition prevalent throughout the country that:

> The day that you see Christopher's face,
> That day shall you not die an evil death.

This had the effect of causing large representations of the Saint to be painted on the wall near the porch where he could be visited daily. It is the same Saint (the patron of travellers) whose image was carried by the Yeoman, and he reappears today as a medallion for the dashboard of a motor-car.

The giant Christopher here in the village of Slapton in Northamptonshire (**82**) is quite well preserved. The fishes underfoot are the artist's way of suggesting that the

82 *St Christopher (a Mural)*

83 *A 'Doom' Painting*

Saint is wading through water. Notice the mermaid admiring herself in a mirror. As far as can be ascertained such pictures showing the Christ-carrier were displayed in roughly two hundred English churches.

The most important of all medieval wall-paintings was the 'Doom' or Last Judgement, with its scene of Heaven and Hell. It became an opportunity for satire if any of the Hell-people on the left hand of God the Father could be identified with living people. In painting such a large scene, made of a number of small and simultaneous ones, the artists may have had visual recourse to the conventions of religious play-staging, since the Last Day was the climax of the mystery cycles shown in many of our major cities in the fourteenth century.

None of the Dooms, situated high above the church chancel, is especially suitable for a single photographic plate. It is generally agreed that the finest of all is that in

St Thomas's Church, Salisbury, but that will be found in M. D. Anderson's invaluable *The Imagery of British Churches*. The photograph here is from Wenhaston in Suffolk, where the Doom is in only a moderate state of preservation (**83**). Christ is shown seated on the rainbow, with two saints who witness the division of human kind. The lucky ones are finely characterized as blissful creatures being led into a small fortification. Note the attempt to segregate the sexes, however. The second panel shows St Peter receiving four souls: a bishop and three crowned heads. For the third panel the artist shows a pair of balances operated by an angel and a devil, in which a soul could be weighed and found wanting. Various damned souls are in the offing. At the right of the picture note the outlines of a pair of huge jaws. The damned are being herded into the traditional concept of the Hell Mouth as it appeared on the stage during the mystery cycle performances: the jaws of a huge sea-monster.

Visitors to old churches should always look for traces of colour on the walls. Failing any frescoes one can often find carvings or even scratchings which abound in certain churches. For example, the church at Ashwell in Hertfordshire has a remarkable quantity of scratchings. These include an identifiable outline of Old St Paul's in London and insulting phrases in Latin ('the corners are not joined; I spit at them') and culminate in a tragic message to the world from the plague-stricken and tempest-tossed world of the mid-fourteenth century that is shown and translated on pp. 108–9. These examples of graffiti may be multiplied indefinitely.

We now continue the survey of decorative schemes inside medieval churches with a glance at the specimen of stained glass (**84**). It is a theological window which puts the regular pastoral work of the Church into vitreous form. The practical nature of this set of illustrations makes it far more significant than a series of saints' figures. It shows the Seven Sacraments which are the mainsprings of the Church's mission. Such a series is often to be found carved round the pediment of a font but these are not often in so fine a state as the glass panels from the church at Doddiscombleigh in Devon, where all except the Christ figure are medieval.

At the top left-hand corner is the *Mass*. The priest is elevating the Host above his head, preparatory to receiving it himself and then distributing others to the congregation. The chalice with the wine remains on the altar to be offered up next.

Below is *Matrimony*, with the couple offering their hands to be joined by the priest. Nothing in this picture shows that this part of the ceremony usually took place at the church door (we recall the Wife of Bath's over-indulgence: 'Husbondes at churche door she hadde five').

At the foot of the left panel is seen the sacrament of *Confirmation* which is administered only by a bishop. Here he seems to be in outdoor habit, with a stole round his shoulder and a mitre on his head. It is an infant receiving the sacrament.

84 *A Seven Sacrament Window*

Beneath the figure of Christ is *Penance*. The penitent is in full view of others as he is confessing. Since there were no pews in churches before the end of the fourteenth century it is not surprising to find no indication of a confessional box in any representation of this sacrament.

Holy Orders, also administered by a bishop in his complete ceremonial vestments, is at the head of the right-hand column. He lays his hand upon the head of each supplicant in turn and after this they celebrate their own first Mass and take up the duties of the priesthood.

Baptism shows a priest evidently about to immerse the infant. The parents and a godparent are identifiable, while the parish clerk holds the book open for the priest to read the prayers.

Last in the sequence should come *Extreme Unction*, the anointing of the dying, known as the last rites of the Church. But in fact the window shows us a scene in which the priest is giving the sick man the last Communion. He is holding a paten from which the sick man has taken the Host. The man holding the candle is the clerk and the others are the relatives.

The connexion of all these sacraments with Christ is traceable in the series of red lines that rise from Christ's five wounds and convey divine grace in the officiation and reception of each.

Apart from the debate on marriage which is conducted by many of the pilgrim-narrators, it is not surprising to find that the references to sacraments are restricted in *The Canterbury Tales*. Penance is one of the Friar's best gambits, and his method of ingratiating himself with the best people in the town. It is unconventional, however, to find a satirical treatment of Extreme Unction in the *Summoner's Tale*, and a corpse in the *Prioress's Tale* which refuses to be silent and lie down when it is brought into the church.

More deeply engaging is the evidence we have from this series of related scenes of the systematic way of thinking, an ordered and enumerated one, which dominated the Church's thought. It has been said by an art critic, Arnold Hauser, that Gothic art, with its insistence on the many parallels, branches and images intended to be read both separately and together, is a form which 'leads the onlooker from one detail to another and causes him . . . to "unravel" the successive parts of the work one after the other.' The better we get to know Chaucer's *Tales* the more we are likely to agree. Hauser has also made the following most relevant comment which applies to all the popular images that may be used to elucidate the work of Chaucer: 'Whether the individual work is made up of several comparatively independent parts or is not analysable into such parts, where it is a pictorial or a plastic, an epic or a dramatic representation, it is always the principle of expansion and not of concentration, of co-ordination and not of sub-ordination, of the open sequence and not of the closed geometrical form by which it is dominated. The successive panes of a large window are especially adapted to the intricacies of theological exposition. Thus, the windows revealing the labours of the months, the sins and virtues or the sacraments are especially suitable to the teaching schemes of the medieval parish priest looking round his church for lessons for a sermon.'

Before passing on to the representation of the Seven Deadly Sins it should be noted that the number 7 had an especial fascination for the medieval mind. There was held

85 *Pride*

86 *Covetousness*

to be a central all-connecting idea behind the fact that there were seven sacraments, deadly sins, contrary virtues, planets, gifts of the Holy Ghost and petitions of the Lord's Prayer. Nor was 7 the only number. The 3 of the Trinity offers an immediate parallel and the enumeration of 5 in the device of the pentangle in *Sir Gawain and the Green Knight* is a further example of the dependence of poetry upon the formulae of religious art in this period. The elaboration in that poem opens thus:

> First he was funden fautles in his five wittes,
> And efte failed never the freke[1] in his five fingres,
> And alle his afiaunce[2] upon folde[3] was in the five woundes
> That Cryst kaght on the croys, as the crede telles;
> And where-so-ever this mon in melly[4] was stad,[5]
> His thro thoght was in that, thurgh alle other thinges,
> That alle his fersnes[6] he feng[7] at the five joyes
> That the hende[8] heven quene had of hir childe.

The most popular form of enumeration was undoubtedly that of the Sins. The *Parson's Tale* is a sermon on the Sins, showing all their ramifications, and allowing the hearers to ponder on their own place in this scheme which the medieval Church

[1] man. [2] trust. [3] earth. [4] contest. [5] placed. [6] courage. [7] received. [8] courteous.

87 *Lechery with Chastity*

worked out so carefully and elaborated in regular courses of sermons. The illustrations have been taken from manuscripts and from church carvings in order to suggest that the work of the church was pervaded from roof to floor with the need to combat sin and offer virtue in its stead.

Pride always stands at the head of the list and is illustrated in a wood-carving of distinction from the Suffolk church of Blythburgh (**85**). A glance shows that the pride is mainly in apparel. The folds of the dress, the *liripipe* hat, add character to the work and provide the preacher with material ready to hand about the excessive money and thought that goes into the wardrobe. The Wife of Bath is one of Chaucer's examples of this defect and it is noteworthy that only the Squire outpaces her in this matter.

Covetousness, from the same sequence, is also a dramatic character (**86**). Notice the money-box he is sitting on and the open hands. For a counterpart in *The Canterbury Tales* the Doctor of Physic springs to mind with his hankering after 'gold in physik'.

For *Lust* or *Lechery* looking drunken in green velvet we have gone to an illuminated manuscript of the *Parson's Tale* itself (**87**). *Lust* is seated on a goat, the animal symbol of lust, while the sparrow perched on her finger is its bird symbol. On the right hand is the figure of *Chastity* looking on in disgust at the intoxicated creature before her. She is standing on a lion and has the halo and mien of an angel. Her cross seems to have transfixed the lion.

Anger is represented from a different medium. It is a picture of a king who has to be restrained by his counsellors, a roof boss in Norwich Cathedral of the raging Herod

88 *Anger*

(**88**). The scene shows Herod as he was acted in mystery plays, where his anger and hysteria were always acted for more than they were worth, reminding us of Hamlet's phrase 'out-herods Herod'.

Gluttony is seated on a bear and intent upon eating a small songbird which in its turn is eating an infinite worm. *Abstinence*, with a lily for chastity and what looks like a coffee-pot (undoubtedly full of water), offers the reader of the manuscript a hint of better spiritual life (**89**).

Envy (*Invidia*), with a dagger to 'stab in the back', is riding a cat, while *Charity* is bearing the Sacred Heart (**90**). Perhaps the finest of this series is the Blythburgh carving of *Sloth* (**91**). He is caught sitting in bed, and obviously reluctant to leave it. The skilled craftsman was able to imitate the rumpled blankets. The outstretched hands seem inert and passive.

It is possible to find traces of all the sins or their opposing virtues in *The Canterbury Tales* and for an understanding of what they meant to the churchgoer of the period one has only to read the appropriate portions of the *Parson's Tale* or the *Pardoner's Tale*. One thinks of the Lust of Nicholas in the *Miller's Tale*, the Anger of the Reeve after he has heard that same *Tale*, the faction and strife created between the Friar and the Summoner, the pride and sensuality of the Wife of Bath. One counterbalances it with pictures of spiritual zeal in the *Second Nun's Tale* and the *Prioress's Tale*. It was not Chaucer's purpose to give a perfect Gothic gallery of the Deadly Sins, but they were inevitably part of his vision of life. For a more didactic use of this sequence one turns

89 *Gluttony with Abstinence*

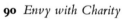

90 *Envy with Charity*

91 *Sloth*   **92** *Grotesque from Lincoln Cathedral*

to *Piers Plowman* with its evocations of popular life and theological truth blended perfectly together, as in this study of Avarice:

> He was bitelbrowed and baberlipped also,
> With two blered eyghen as a blynde hagge;
> And as a letheren purs lolled his chekes,
> Wel sydder[1] than his chin thei chiveled[2] for elde.[3]
> And as a bondman of his bacoun his berd was bidraveled.

One's immediate response, of course, is that the pictures are grotesque but meaningful. There is an aesthetic idea behind them. An exaggeration of the outward appearances of evil warns the reader of the complementary inner wickedness. It is not done for the purpose of shocking and titillating, for a great amount of evil and bawdiness in medieval poetry has the pursuit of the good as its ideal. In the exaggerated grotesqueness of Chaucer's Miller and Summoner, for instance, the same philosophy is at work. The boorish bluntness of one and the frightening face of the other stand out like

[1] lower.   [2] quivered.   [3] age.

gargoyles on the parapet of a church, or the half-men half-beast images that decorate the margins of manuscripts of the period: conceived with a fundamentally moral purpose no matter how amusing their repulsiveness may appear.

This quality is illustrated in the grotesque from Lincoln Cathedral (**92**). It is a devil figure with a wide-open mouth suitable for a water-spout but not now connected with the guttering. The snake's tail round the body completes the image and in the first detail it recalls Chaucer's portrait of the Miller:

> His mouth as greet was as a greet forneys.

And that *forneys* is in hell.

THE PLOWMAN

93 *Ploughing*

Depriving the Plowman of a tale Chaucer left him an idealized figure and denied him the actuality that strikes us in the portrait of his brother, the Parson. Why he should remain a symbol rather than an individual has been discussed in connexion with the miniature on p. 24. If we need a more human picture of peasants and ploughmen we turn to the series of monthly labours on p. 20 in which the men are attractively characterized, or to the well-known picture above (**93**).

The plough in this scene is heavy, made of wood and shod with metal; it needs four oxen to drag it and every detail of its construction comes out of the painting. The men in hoods and gowns look hardened, while the oxen have a human sense of suffering endurance upon their faces. This picture has a perfect verbal counterpart from a contemporary writer. It speaks of the work of the ploughman who 'yoketh them and maketh them draw the plough, and pricketh the slow with the goad and maketh them draw even; and pleaseth them with whistling and song to make them bear the yoke with better will for liking the melody of his voice.'

The Plowman, as Chaucer presents him, is a symbol of 'pees and parfit charitee', of the ungrudging labour of the Third Estate. He also obeys the mandate laid down for his class of man in the *Chess Book* by Jacobus de Cessolis, already referred to, where he is one of the pawns: 'and first the labourer of the erthe ought to knowe his god that formed and made heven and erthe of noughte, And ought to have loyaulte and trouth in hymself And despise deth for to entende to his laboure.'

In all these details the Plowman is a counterpart of the far more symbolic Piers Plowman, hero of the long poem of that name by William Langland, Chaucer's contemporary. In that poem, too, the land-worker is an instrument of salvation to the community, not only in the agricultural but also in the spiritual sense. From Langland's poem a reader draws a great deal of the theology of the period, together with many satirical sketches of contemporary life. In an effort to understand the life of the medieval peasant one quotation stands out, offering a contrast to the life of the gentry. In an interview with Hunger, Piers says:

> I haue no peny, quod Piers, poletes forto bigge,[1]
> Ne neyther gees ne grys[2] but two grene cheses,
> A fewe cruddes and creem and an hauer[3] cake,
> And two loues of benes and bran ybake for my fauntis;[4]
> And yet I sey, by my soule I have no salt bacoun,
> Ne no kokeney,[5] bi Cryst coloppes[6] forto maken.

That was the diet of the English land-worker: beans, bacon, eggs, cheese, a little milk. Add to it a few other vegetables, and apples and pears when in season. In the winter he would have had considerably less.

In the latter part of the fourteenth century there came the evidence of rural discontent. Under Wat Tyler and the priest John Ball the peasants in the Home Counties marched and converged on London. They demanded a clear improvement in their lot and a great deal of violence took place in which many people were put to death. Chaucer's protector, John of Gaunt, escaped their hands because he had left London. It remains a problem for the reader whether the Revolt of 1381 conditioned Chaucer's attitude to the peasantry. It may be thought that he offered his Plowman as a didactic portrait of how peasants *should* behave rather than as a report on how they actually behaved. For whatever reason Chaucer's Plowman is not an individual person strongly etched in our minds.

In this scene John Ball is preaching to Waltre le Fieulier or Wat Tyler. Note that the rebels display the banners of England and St George, for they maintained their loyalty to the Crown throughout their rising (**94**). When hostile groups are drawn from the same country there must be many scores on which they are in T. S. Eliot's words 'united in the strife that divided them'. The Revolt failed, but it was not forgotten or entirely

---

[1] buy. [2] porkers. [3] oat. [4] infants. [5] scullion. [6] stews.

94 *The Peasants' Revolt*

dismissed. Wat Tyler and his associate Jack Straw did not bring about the enfranchise-
ment of workers through their onslaughts. They caused a great deal of alarm in the
country and Chaucer remembered the confusion they caused in the *Nun's Priest's Tale*:

> Certes, he Jakke Straw and his meynee
> Ne made nevere shoutes half so shrille
> Whan that they wolden any Fleming kille.

Nor did John Ball, who saw himself leading the Church to a new spiritual height,
attain anything. The rising was suppressed and the leaders put to death. Richard II
himself stood up to the demands, seemed to concede them, and with consummate
knavery went back on his word. The Peasants' Revolt needed centuries to attain its
goal, but with the electoral reforms of the nineteenth century something similar was at
last attained.

The Miller, the chief buffoon of the party, is shown as Chaucer intended, with his bagpipe and his blue surcoat, a rough lout with a heavy sword and no evidence of grace anywhere in him (**95**).

His trade was familiar to all cottagers because it was essential for every family to have its corn ground at the local windmill (or water-mill) which was the property of the lord of the manor. The miller himself became one of the village's most hated characters because he tended so often to give short measure. In his treatment of the Miller, the poet was once again turning common attitude into poetical character. There is something of the gargoyle in the verbal portrait and the Lincoln gargoyle on p. 127 catches the poet's vision perfectly.

The mill itself is most sensitively painted (**96**). It is a more opulent establishment than the one we imagine Robin himself operated. The water-wheel is a piece of apparatus that has not changed with the times, so that the scene does not date as many of the other miniatures of popular life have done.

95 *The Miller*

96 *A Water-mill*

The Miller is also gifted as a story-teller, when he is drunk. Still more, he is an actor, and was engaged to rant the role of Pilate in the mystery play of the Passion. The roof boss of Herod being restrained, symbol of Anger (**88**), is a reflection of the style of acting. It may also be noticed that the old carpenter in his tale is a grotesque parody of Noah, also the subject of a popular play; it is also a great deal more of a poetic entity than one would expect from such a narrator and Chaucer seems to have felt an attachment to his Miller that he could never feel for that other drunkard, the Summoner.

Since bagpipers were traditional nuisances the small cartoon of a deathly visitant confronting a piper needs no further explanation (**97**).

97 *A Bagpiper*

98 *The Reeve*

THE REEVE

Oswald, the Reeve, lived in isolation and he kept to the rear of the pilgrimage (**98**). In his own *Prologue* he is revealed as an aged lecher, and everything in his portrait suggests the abhorrence that villagers felt for him, either as a power in the region or as a dark and frightening individual.

The hood and shoulder cape are those of peasants of the period: he is not exhibiting his superiority in his manner of dress. That comes within. He knows how to defraud his overlord (possibly an absentee landowner who has gone to the city and left Oswald in charge) as well as to outwit the peasants.

The miniature of the overseer on the harvest-field is a perfect illustration of the work of a reeve (**99**). Note the balance of the pictorial composition perfectly adapted to the available space.

In his dark fearful nature he is both choleric and saturnine—coming under the inner influence of one force and the external power of the other. From the pages of Bartolomaeus we read that Saturn 'maketh a man broun and fowle, mysdoynge, slowe and

99 *The Reeve in the Field*

100 *Saturn and his Children*

101 *'The sheep hath paid for all'*

hevy, eleynge[1] and sory—seldome gladde and merye or laghynge. . . . [They] ben yelowe of colour, and broun of heere and sharpe in all the body, and unsemely. And ben not skoynous[2] of foule and stynkynge clothynge. And he lovyth stynkyng beestes and unclene soure thynge and skarp. For of theyr complexyon Melancolyke humour hathe maystry.' Chaucer, however, preferred to make the Reeve choleric, contrary to tradition, crossing thus the medieval fluid barrier. This passage has indeed the correct note for a man peasants hated 'as the deeth'.

The Saturn scene from the *Hausbuch* offers most violent images (**100**). The corpse swings on a gibbet, another has been broken on the wheel; a third is being led to execution; a peasant is in the stocks, a butcher is slaughtering a horse. Saturn was also a god of agriculture and the villagers can continue nonchalantly ditching and ploughing, no matter what is happening to other members of the community.

In the *Knight's Tale* Saturn lets loose the most potent evil upon the world. The description of his temple is not a gallery of pictures but a series of ideas based on the pain of the world's evil. Saturn says:

> Myn is the drenching in the see so wan;
> Myn is the prison in the derke cote;
> Myn is the strangling and hanging by the throte.

Returning from the symbolic qualities of the Reeve to the practical work in which he excelled, it is more pleasant to give prominence to the sheep that were always in his reckoning. This is a beautiful study in semi-human expression as if the animals regarded themselves as the pride of the countryside. In truth, this is what they became in the later Middle Ages. As the sources of millions of fleeces every year, they provided the basis of English economic security. They also yielded lambskin fur, mutton, milk and cheese, while the oily wool on their bellies was employed for medical purposes. Although not perhaps as essential as the camel to the Arab, the sheep was the source of some of the huge fortunes which financed the great secular and religious architecture of the period. Here they receive an understanding illuminator (**101**). The presence of the women indicates another product: ewes' milk. The sheep remain the central attraction.

[1] wretched.   [2] ashamed.

It was a magnificent stroke to lead right through the gallery of pilgrims to this last pair. The Summoner (or Apparitor) and the Pardoner (or Quaestor), bosom companions, are shown to be equally corrupted and more than a little insane. There is no shred of equivocation in the portraits. Though they would have been a shame to any profession, as officials of the Church they are despicable symbols of evil.

102 *The Summoner*

THE SUMMONER: HELL

The Summoner's madness is shown in the portrait (**102**) by his garland and the large flat loaf that he has girt to him like a shield. His repulsive skin condition can just be detected in the painting, though no picture can do justice to the results of his diet of leeks, onions, garlic and red wine, all of which were forbidden to those suffering with a skin condition bordering on leprosy. In his hand he is offering a sealed writ of excommunication, a symbol of his craft, but here derisive.

103 *Hell*. Pol de Limbourg

The images of wine and food do not make him a Bacchanalian figure—far from it, since that implies vitality. Nor is this an example of the grotesque as with the Miller, since there is nothing comic. The heart of the portrait is fiery, burning with skin infections, and inflamed as if loosed from Hell. To underline his point more obviously Chaucer makes a summoner the central figure in the *Friar's Tale*. This man on his rounds meets another who comes from 'fer in the north contree' and turns out to be Satan.

The Hell scene (**103**) comes from the Duc de Berri's Book of Hours and is in total contrast with previous reproductions taken from it. Pol de Limbourg has here shown all manner of victims including some with the tonsure. They are being dragged, hurled and belched across the page by horned devils, while the master devil is enjoying a roasting temperature. In such a background the Summoner with his countenance 'sawcefleem' is seen as perfectly at home.

THE PARDONER: DEATH

The artist has interpreted the Pardoner correctly (**104**). The vernicle on his cap—a small badge with the face of Christ embroidered on it in commemoration of the kerchief carried by St Veronica and with which she wiped Christ's face—is more grotesquely out of place when the whole man is seen. The effect is not unlike that of a pirate's cap to our eyes. The cross of latten in the hand may be professional but in this hand is still grimly improbable. The false relics are in the bag round the horse's neck.

The Pardoner's own words are audaciously hypocritical. One looks at such an image as the following with a desire for visual corroboration:

> Thanne peyne I me to strecche forth the nekke,
> And est and west upon the peple I bekke,
> As dooth a dowye sittinge on a berne.

104 *The Pardoner*

A dove—even the Holy Ghost, he thinks. If we turn to the picture of the Preacher Fox on p. 145 there is a better resemblance to elucidate the poetic image.

The *Pardoner's Tale* gains in significance if it is recalled that the two damned souls are the last to be listed in the *General Prologue* and that thoughts should relevantly turn upon Judgement, Heaven and Hell at the end of a sequence of theological ideas.

All over Northern Europe especially, painters were commissioned to depict the power of Death. In some examples there was but a single memento of it, as on p. 140. In many there were assemblages of these individual figures, each confronted by a skeleton, who were typical of each order of society from the king or emperor downwards. Another favourite motif in medieval painting was the picture of the three live kings who were suddenly confronted by the spectacle of three dead ones. Such a conception could swell to as many as forty individual deaths always returning at the last to the words of the preacher. The feasting scene on p. 91 conveys a little of the same quality of diabolic retribution for sin.

In Northern Europe very little of this tradition remains in paintings that date back before the fifteenth century, but the works within this convention carry on after the Reformation. The sequence by Hans Holbein (1538) is possibly the best of all, and the most appropriate one to illustrate the *Pardoner's Tale* is used as the frontispiece to the Cambridge edition. It is known that there were medieval plays on the subject and in the evolution of drama one can point to the tragedies of Marlowe and consider the influence of the late medieval death traditions there too. In *Edward II* the victim is an English king, in *Tamburlaine*, a world conqueror, and in *Dr Faustus*, a highly significant scholar. Finally, Cyril Tourneur's play *The Revenger's Tragedy* succeeds in suggesting the corruption and death of an entire society still within the framework of the morality play tradition.

This is enough to suggest the width and scope of the medieval preoccupation with death in its various art forms. We must return to examples which speak from Chaucer's day, even though the pictorial examples have largely disappeared. In the *Pardoner's Tale* Death comes in the form of a heap of coins—the Old Man is not Death but only a man with an urge to submit himself to the medieval 'death-wish'. More powerful because it suggests a collective death is the following passage from *Piers Plowman*:

> Death came dryving after and al to douste paschte[1]
> Kynges and knyghtes caysers[2] and popes;
> Lered ne lewede he lefte no man stande;
> That he hitte evene sterede never after.
> Many a lovely lady and her lemmanes[3] knyghtes
> Sounede[4] and swelte for sorwe of Deths dyntes.

Behind such lines one can detect the influence of a sequence of pictures or a mystery play. The play of the Last Judgement in the Chester Mystery Cycle might well be read as a literary parallel.

[1] pasted.   [2] kaisers, emperors.   [3] lovers.   [4] swooned.

105 *Death calls for the Bishop*

The illustration of Death and the Bishop is a particularly fine one (**105**). Like Everyman in the play of that name, the victim, a robed Bishop, shrinks from the coming of Death in a shroud. Note the chess-board. The photograph comes from a window in

106 *A Tomb and Cadaver*

St Andrew's Church, Norwich, where there were once other windows, now destroyed, which may conceivably have returned to the chess-board and death motifs. As it stands isolated from its original sequence it illustrates the figure of Death turning upon the corruption inside the Church and revealing himself as no friend to any Bishop, Pardoner or Summoner who shrinks from the last things: Death, Judgement, Heaven and Hell.

The last picture in this chapter is of a tomb with a cadaver upon it (**106**). It is a product of a time (about 1400) when people were more and more aware of the terrors of death and left their tombs as reminders to passers-by of the slenderness of the attractions of the world and the need to prepare for the next state of man.

There is no more potent representation of the figure of Death from the year 1400 than this one at Feniton in Devon. The body is deposited in the stone tomb and on the top is a duplicate of the wasting rotting corpse packed into an enclosed space in the church wall as if to simulate the boxed-in nature of the tomb itself. Note that the folds of the shroud are thrown back to expose the cadaver whose face is now featureless though his ears and his hair retain their former shape. In fact, the perfectly straight hair-style—what we might call a 'Henry V cut'—is an agreeable feature still. All over Europe such gruesome reminders of the imminence of death in the Middle Ages will be encountered by the modern pilgrim.

It has been said that we can judge the strength or weakness of any period by its attitude towards death. Here there is a perfect realism which expects all later ages to share the same firmness of mind by exhibiting the one certain thing in life, which is death.

THE NUN'S PRIEST

The Nun's Priest is no more than a name in the *General Prologue* : in fact he is only one of three priests in the company of the Prioress and the Second Nun. Some writers have thought these priests were chaplains and wondered why so many were necessary; others have interpreted them as bodyguards for the ladies:

> See, which braunes hath this gentil preest,
> So gret a nekke, and swich a large breest.

The Host's remarks are contradicted by the elegant and rather boyish subject of the Ellesmere miniature (**107**). It is also quite inaccurate as a representation of these comments:

> What thogh thyn hors be bothe foul and lene?
> If he wol serve thee, rekke nat a bene.

The illuminator had little to go upon, but he failed to observe what lines were laid down for his guidance.

107 *The Nun's Priest*

108 *February.* Pol de Limbourg

Fortunately, in such a book as the present it is his famous *Tale* that should be illustrated and not his character and function in convent life. The *Tale* is divided between the daily routine of the widow and her small household and the dramatic events of the Cock and the Fox. The French illustration is one of the most fortunate of all coincidences. It is the February page of the Duc de Berri's famous Book of Hours (**108**).

Three peasants and their cat are warming themselves at the fire. The scene is perfectly realistic (except that a wall is removed to let us see them). The wooden structure of a peasant's cottage is laid bare. Wattle fencing encloses the yard and the sheep are under cover. A little group of magpies has flown down in search of food: they must be accepted as substitutes for the Cock and his seven hens. Beehives stand in the corner to recall the final scene of Chaucer's *Tale*:

> Out of the hive cam the swarm of bees.

The man chopping wood for the fire, another blowing on his hands to keep warm, the pack-donkey and the tall cylindrical dovecot are all typical of village life. It shows the vividness and humanity of Chaucer's story and brings it to life as if it were intended for the purpose. Aquarius and Pisces, signs of the zodiac, are overhead and all astronomical details are complete.

The widow is Chaucer's best portrait of a poor woman. Her small sooty house in the tale recalls a passage in Froissart's *Chronicles*. In the year 1382 the Earl of Flanders had to flee from the mob and found just such another cottage: 'only a small house, dirty and smoky, and as black as jet: there was only in this place one poor chamber, over which was a sort of garret that was entered by means of a ladder of seven steps, where on a miserable bed, the children of this poor woman lay.' For Chaucer's evidence of such conditions we read:

> Ful sooty was hire bour and eek hir halle,
> In which she eet ful many a sklendre meel.

The main subject came to Chaucer from folk-lore. A great cycle of animal stories was known orally throughout Europe and written down in several languages. In France there was the *Roman de Renard* in which fox-cunning was exemplified time after time. In England the theme was often pursued in pictorial form, but Chaucer's is by far the best example of a Fox story of the period.

The wood-carving of a pew-end in Brent Knoll Church, Somerset, shows one of the favourite themes in medieval churches (**109**). Reynard the Fox is preaching to the birds. He has, as you see, the habit of a bishop, and was to be taken as a comic satire on bishops and other preachers. Their congregations appear as bird-witted folk filling every branch to listen. The purpose of the Fox's sermon is ultimately to devour his listeners. Out of a similar legend Ben Jonson took his comedy, *Volpone*, in which the protagonist

109 *The Fox preaching*

is a human fox ensnaring with false promises of large inheritance a group of people with bird names who come to see him as he lies shamming death. The scene of the Fox shamming death immediately prior to striking out at victims is also found in popular carvings of Chaucer's time. In the same series from which this fine one is taken there is another showing Reynard dead, strung up on a rope. Note the foot of this church bench upon which a carcase is being roasted on a spit.

The sequence of animal illuminations from about the year 1300 continue the Fox story (**110–113**). In the manner reminiscent of the nursery rhyme 'Who killed Cock

110 *The Dog-piper*   **111** *The Goat*

Robin?' some of the animals attend his funeral. Music being an essential here as at every other formal medieval occasion, it is provided by a dog-piper. Look more closely at the picture (**110**) and you notice that it is really a cat which forms the bag, giving substance to the popular idea that a bagpipe's sound resembles the noise of a scalded cat. The goat, solemn and stupid, carries the cross and has contrived to arrange his coat to look like an ecclesiastical robe (**111**).

Near by at a small, fantastic church with a vast rose-window set too low in the wall the donkey tolls the bell (**112**). The central figure of this ceremony is carried by the cat and the stag (**113**). The corpse is draped but nose and tail peep out. It is impossible to say if he is really dead. One can only say that in accordance with the legend he did die having caused the deaths of so many others:

> My lord youre fader—God his soule blesse—
> And eek youre mooder, of hire gentillesse,
> Han in myn hous ybeen to my greet ese;

Chaucer catches the politeness and the menace with notable subtlety. It was a tale already well known, so that the artist is challenged to add new overtones of courtesy and craftiness to make the Fox both animal and human at once.

Such scenes of the animal world serve to remind the reader of the large numbers of wild animals then living in England. They all exerted great fascination over the minds

112 *The Donkey*

of artists and sculptors who painted or carved them, even some whose like they had never seen. It is one of the delights of old churches to find evidence of such animal legends: to discover oddly malformed camels and elephants, for instance, as well as animals that everybody knew. Animals and man shared the creation together and in their perfectly natural way had lessons to offer civilized man. There was a kind of class

113 *The Corpse*

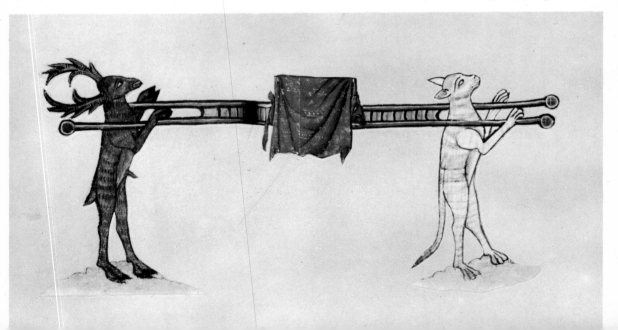

distinction that could be discerned among them as well. In his *Parliament of Fowls* Chaucer mirrored the class-divisions in human society in the similar divisions of bird-life. Only in the *Nun's Priest's Tale* did he develop the possibilities of such a comparison, and the pictures of domestic and animal life that he placed in juxtaposition are continued in these illustrations.

THE CANON'S YEOMAN

The Canon's Yeoman is more of an afterthought than the Nun's Priest, because he is a sudden arrival on the Pilgrim's Way, panting after them on his horse. He is shown as a bleary-eyed, overheated man in the poem; in the miniature (**114**) he may seem heated but he is altogether too neat and scholarly for the poor distraught laboratory steward who tells his story in great gasps and rushes of feeling. He seems to have a hole in the knee of his hose, and the empty bag on the horse's back is one of the things about him that attracts the Host's attention—as a landlord he may be used to absconding people without luggage—and in the interchanges between the two, Chaucer shows not only how inquisitive the Host is but—by extension—his own method of questioning characters in order to reach a judgement upon behaviour.

The fascination of alchemy as a pseudo-science needs no explanation. The end-product eagerly sought, sweeping all other considerations before it, is the possession of the elixir or the philosopher's stone which would transmute iron to gold or secure personal immortality on earth and a great wealth of other spiritual powers. In a later form the desire took upon itself the symbol of Dr Faust, familiar from legend and play.

114 *The Canon's Yeoman*

The Alchemist's Laboratory

At a lower level the pursuit was conducted in a laboratory with crucibles, flasks and retorts being subjected to a dozen processes of cooling, heating, mixing, heating, cooling and heating again. Each step had its own technique and its margin of error as well as a technical name: calcination, solution, separation, conjunction, putrefaction, congelation, cibation, sublimation, fermentation, exaltation, multiplication and projection. Either in every step or only in the last—the projection of the liquid upon base metal which would transmute it into gold—the experiments always failed but always left hope for the optimist that the search was almost complete. The Yeoman's view of alchemy is a great deal more humble, mundane and particular. He is concerned with keeping the laboratory tidy and stoking up the fires.

The laboratory scene gives a sense of reality to the tale (**115**). In the centre is a retort standing on a pile of bricks to receive the distillations of the flask on the

116 *Mercury and his Children*

three-legged stool. The containers on the top of the oven have the appearance of birds with long beaks and were called pelicans. A chimney for the escape of fumes was the prime need when the emphasis was so strongly upon different intensities of heat. On the other side of the laboratory are more pieces of apparatus, an astronomical chart and what appears to be a puffball fish suspended from the ceiling. The table and books indicate the amount of reading and writing that made alchemy a highly specialized study and an esoteric art demanding a lifetime's adaptation.

Basically, it was thought that metals were anxious to improve their status but were, like mankind, forced into a rigid social pattern of their own in which Gold as the Sun replaced Gold as the king's crown or the godhead itself. Yet, in order to conduct the experiments successfully, it was necessary to plot the influences of the other planets. In mankind it was natural to consider their relation with ill-health: there was nothing more desirable than to allocate the chemical elements to the planetary gods as well:

> Sol gold is, and Luna silver we threpe,
> Mars iren, Mercurie quiksilver we clepe,
> Saturnus leed, and Juppiter is tin,
> And Venus coper, by my fader kin.

It is now evident that alchemy is only a part of the connected chain of correspondences that ruled the universe: if one only held the key one could turn back the sun, move the stars in their rounds and become master of the globe. It was this aspect of the craft of alchemy that exercised the strongest power over its adherents. The tutelary god of alchemy was Mercury, whose name was given to that tantalizing substance, half-metal, half-liquid, that features so largely in experiments.

Mercury, as depicted in the *Hausbuch* illustration, is a great deal more benign than the other planets (**116**). The scenes on earth of people of mercurial temperament include no violence, even though the god was also a patron of sneak-thieves. Here it is his power over the lesser creative imagination that is given pictorial form. In the bottom left-hand corner is an alchemist at work. Grouped as if in one vast workshop of the world are craftsmen of all sorts: a turnsmith, a clock- and instrument-maker, a manuscript copyist (scrivener), an organ-builder, a mason, a painter working on an altarpiece and a sculptor working on a statue strapped to a bench. In the bottom right-hand corner is shown either the art of gastronomy or merely a break for refreshments. One slightly discordant note is introduced by the cries of the schoolboy being chastised. This scene is common in medieval art where it is sometimes used as a symbol of Anger: the teacher has probably carefully explained that he does it more out of Sorrow. And Mercury above looks complacently upon his children; the trappings seem to make a polypod out of his horse and everybody born under his aegis is thought to be most fortunate.

117 *Cosmological Scene*

Because alchemy is not an isolated subject but part of the wider scrutiny of the nature of the universe that was to bear fruit during the Renaissance, the picture of medieval man trying to penetrate the hidden secrets fits pertinently into this chapter (**117**). Sun, moon and stars are shown in their orbs and the man is delving into reaches of outer space where the wheels of Ezekiel's vision are turning and spare planets and clouds are stored. It was firmly believed that there was a background of this type to the universe. The effect is one of the workings of a vast machinery. The full acceptance of modern cosmology with its theory of continuous rotation had not dawned in the Middle Ages although ideas bearing upon it had been introduced into Europe in the thirteenth century. Once a man saw the possibilities of magnetic force and later of gravity he was no longer imprisoned in the idea of individual malevolent forces in the different planets. Such a cosmology could only point towards a single universal god.

Medieval thinking, based on the planets, the humours and the signs of the zodiac, was perfectly consistent, even if it did nothing to encourage a more scientific direction of thought. It is too easy to despise what was done and to forget that the theory of correspondences and influences, more magical than scientific, was in its own way a highly developed art. The findings of the alchemists probably suggested more profitable lines of thinking than the practice of medicine. Further progress in the sciences is not in the world of Chaucer at all, in spite of his own interest in the science of astronomy, apparent in many of his poems. For Chaucer, the system of man was locked in the system of the universe, and treated as something magical, rather than scientific, in origin. The interlocking consistency of the theories is remarkable, and so, in general, is the assurance that it was all based upon the work of a creator whose ways were incalculable but to be accepted by mankind. With the scientific renaissance of Elizabeth's time John Donne stated the poet's fear that sun, moon and stars were uncertain of their place, stranded and lost. Yet even in the eighteenth century it was not felt necessary that science should have any claims upon a gentleman's education. Indeed, Edmund Burke spoke disparagingly of what 'geometricians and chemists bring, the one from the dry bones of their diagrams and the other from the soot of their furnaces'.

With the soot of the factory chimneys of the Industrial Revolution poets felt that God had made the country, but that man, in making the town so ugly, had lost sight of him. Only the educated could attempt to rediscover him through the arts or through the mystical nature of such a religion as the restored Roman Catholicism of later nineteenth-century England. The process that began in Chaucer's time is shown to have developed into the conflicts between religion and science and between the alien scientific and artistic cultures discussed in our own century.

For Chaucer, however, the final page of *Troilus and Criseyde* contains the final word:

> Thow oon, and two, and thre, eterne on lyve,
> That regnest ay in thre, and two, and oon,
> Uncircumscript, and al maist circumscrive,
> Us from visible and invisible foon[1]
> Defende, and to thy mercy, everichon,
> So make, us, Jesus, for thi mercy digne,
> For love of mayde and moder thyn benigne.

[1] foes.

It is ironical that Chaucer the pilgrim fell into the hands of the poorer of the two artists working on the Ellesmere manuscripts. Note the little mound underfoot, that artist's trade-mark. He is shown with a belted gown, a *liripipe* hat and perched on a particularly comfortable saddle (**118**). We cannot now discover the actual man who lay behind the painting although in this one case many would give much to know it.

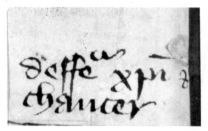

118 *Chaucer*

119 *Chaucer's Autograph*

Even so, there are reasons for attempting to distinguish this Chaucer from the poet of the same name. He entered himself in his own list of pilgrims only to indulge in a little leg-pulling at his own expense. He was a figure in the public service with a reputation for his activities in the Port of London and on different sites controlled by the Royal Works. Born in London at some time after 1340, he advanced to a social height and eminence remarkable for a merchant's son: it has been suggested such a career would have been closed to him if he had been living in most other European countries at that period. Fig. **119** shows his autograph.

120 *John of Gaunt*

The foundation of his success was laid in the Court of Prince Lionel and he moved into the service of Edward III towards the end of the 1360s. From 1374 his name is linked with the Court of John of Gaunt, son of Edward III and uncle of the future monarch, Richard II. From that point until the end of his life the poet enjoyed the favour of Gaunt who was one of the greatest magnates in the country. He wrote *The Book of the Duchess* in memory of Gaunt's first wife, Blanche. During the stormy and tragic period of the 1380s Gaunt suffered through the waxing and waning of royal favour, finally being replaced as Royal Protector by the Duke of Gloucester, and Chaucer suffered with him. The picture of Gaunt may be only a vague likeness (**120**).

It is learned from *The Canterbury Tales* that Chaucer is fat, solitary, elusive and 'elvish' which suggests a sense of humour and a willingness to indulge in private fantasies. If we look at the poet's reactions to his fellow-pilgrims there is a pattern of ambivalence about them. As we have already noted, he seems to have enjoyed the presence and company of some of them, while as a moralist he was obliged by a species of 'double-take' to reject some element of their hypocrisy or pretension. This is what happened in the portraits of the Prioress and the Monk, and this is what led him to be less than enthusiastic over the Clerk. He shows a less divided mind, but is still unfair, in portraits such as that of the Manciple where the character dwindles away to nothing. On many of these occasions it is possible to detect that Chaucer, the moralist or poet, failed to back up his twin, the pilgrim; the result does not lead to confusion so much as to richness.

It is one of the themes of this book that Chaucer had all round him visual precedents for what he was doing. The fact that his descriptions of a group of courtiers riding abroad in the springtime or of the movements of animals in a fable can be illustrated from contemporary illuminations is intended to suggest that he was used to conceiving verbal ideas from visual art forms. It is impossible to say how much of the material that he himself saw has since disappeared. Certainly much of it does still exist in many different copies all over Europe. Thus, the picture that shows the old man and the young wife (**50**) responds to the same inspiration as the *Merchant's Tale* and it was such a popular motif that Meckenen did two, and Lucas Cranach no less than five, different studies in the same convention. Chaucer's *Tale* is indebted to other versions written abroad. The conception is international and visual. We are therefore looking at pictures bearing the closest relationship to the poetry, and learning something of the indivisible nature of the arts in medieval Europe. Dancing groups, planetary deities, animal symbols, the signs of the zodiac—signs of both beauty and ugliness in the world—appear in Chaucer's verse as though they were created from a reading of the details in a picture, many of which would have been already familiar to his audience.

Two further views may be hazarded here. One is that the artists of the period were sure that Nature was inimitable, but they could hope, by finding enough of the component parts of a beautiful scene, to put forward the illusion of the natural creation. In the fourteenth century there is no doubt that artists were succeeding. Even the religious pictures take on a more human look. Christ loses some of his grandeur in order to gain humanity. Only at this point can one expect, in carvings and paintings and church architecture, the fullest realization of animal life, the closest resemblance to leaves and fruit. Only at that time could an artist contrive so remarkable a humanity in wood as we have in the characterizations of the Deadly Sins in the church at Blythburgh.

Chaucer himself gave voice to the current view when he wrote of the perfection of the heroine of the *Physician's Tale*:

> As though she wolde seyn, 'Lo ! I, Nature,
> Thus kan I forme and peynte a creature,
> Whan that me list; who kan me countrefete?
> Pigmalion noght, though he ay forge and bete,
> Or grave, or peynte.

Yet it was in the nature of the verbal art as well as the visual that the practitioner should try.

It is known that writers followed rules laid down for composition and studied models in order to achieve what was expected of them by the rhetoricians. In these books of models outlines of many different conventions will be found: how to describe a lady, a horse, a king, a landscape. The scholar Derek Pearsall writes of the scenes of description in *Sir Gawain and the Green Knight* in words that might apply to the winter journey in the *Franklin's Tale*. He says: 'The poet does not describe the winter in the mountains because he is fond of wild, romantic scenery and wants us to share his pleasure in it, but because the narrative demands at this point an illustration of the discomforts of Gawain's "anious vyage".' A further comment may be in place. The passages of rhetoric that had been carefully studied and imitated were known as 'colours'. Chaucer's Franklin, who shows himself a master of the elaborate poem, nevertheless admits:

> Colours ne knowe I none, withouten drede.

Yet his poem shows him a liar. The Squire suggests how much there is to learn in the art of poetry and rhetoric:

> I dar nat undertake so heigh a thyng.
> Myn Englissheek is insufficient.
> It moste been a rethor excellent,
> That koude his colours longinge for that art,
> If he sholde hire discriven every part.

In this use of the term 'colours' one finds a reference to the visual arts. Just as one should always look for a rhetorical principle behind any striking piece or verbal art, one can often look with profit and pleasure for a pictorial accompaniment to it which might indeed have served as a model also.

In this book there has been no stress at all upon religious art, apart from ecclesiastical architecture and a few glances at the top or bottom of its decorated pillars. This is because Chaucer preferred secular subject-matter. Nor have we discussed the background of primitive, rough and powerful design that can be felt behind *Sir Gawain* since that too is a separate world. In comparison, Chaucer may well look limited and a little afraid to venture outside his range. For an indication of the artistic parallels that may be found for *Sir Gawain* the reader is invited to turn to an excellent chapter in

Medieval English Poetry by John Speirs, which will be found to enforce the present case for the pictorial models that may have seized upon the writer's imagination. For writings of the period the rule of criticism appears to have been: discover the literary convention which the author is essaying and then judge him for his handling of its swiftness or its slowness, his realization of its several details. The same would be true of the extended use of pictorial conventions in poetry.

The illustrations in this volume show the gaunt, emotional and statuesque painting to be found in the period before Chaucer's birth. They depict the awakening to the humanity of man, the 'animalness' of animals and the 'vegetableness' of trees and flowers: their whole form and essence. They do not draw back from the presence of evil. Indeed, in some of the psalters of the period in particular, they seem to over-emphasize it. The Luttrell Psalter has already been mentioned as a striking example of this. There are many such highly illuminated psalters and prayer-books which offer the best documentation that we have of popular life during the Middle Ages, some of them full of humour and others darker in tone and feeling.

There is, also, and in a class by itself the outstanding example of religious art of the period, the Wilton Diptych (**121**). It combines the functions of royal portrait and altar-piece; though it is housed today in the National Gallery in London it is not a gallery painting. Paintings were mainly confined to churches or to the leaves of manuscripts, although frescoes on walls might take their place in a rich hall.

This painting is composed in two linked panels and was, from its small size, suitable only for a private altar. Compositionally, the two wings of the painting achieve a unity: the figures on the left incline their hands towards the Madonna and Child, while the supernatural ones return the gesture of goodwill to the young monarch.

Richard II came to the throne at a very early age and he is shown here as a boy in a robe of great richness and softness decorated with his personal emblem: the white hart. The same figure is repeated in the medallion on his breast, which is shared with all the angels. All of them wear collars made of jewels and broom-pods, seedcases from a shrub which provided the emblem of the Plantagenet family to which Richard belonged. Three saints standing behind the King are the martyr St Edmund, with his emblematic arrow, St Edward the Confessor with a ring, and St John the Baptist with a lamb. The features of the two saint-kings have been interpreted as those of the King's father and grandfather, the Black Prince and Edward III. Such identification of known people with the saints through symbol or dress, yet still recognized by facial resemblance, is occasionally found in medieval art. One is led to suspect that just as the donors of large altarpieces or stained-glass windows are shown in the pictures themselves, the models of many individual or group portraits would have been recognizable at the date of composition.

121 *The Wilton Diptych*

In the second panel it will be noticed that an angel is carrying the banner of St George as a tribute to the monarch. Note the touching gesture with which the Virgin holds Christ's foot; and the spirituality of his expression. The flowered field on which the heavenly beings stand, their graceful hands, and the background of flame-like wings, are all infinitely delicate.

Although this is not in any way connected with its worth, the picture has proved a puzzle to historians who have been unable to decide the purpose for which it was painted. Some have seen it as a coronation piece for Richard's accession in 1377: others have preferred, on various evidence, to date it later and see it as the memorial of the moment, eleven years later, when Richard held a second coronation to establish his majority and his assumption of full personal rule, freed at last from uncle regents.

It should not seem in the least strange to offer the work of a Flemish artist of the six-teenth century as a last comment on the work of a poet living in England two centuries before. As a swift glance at the pictures shows, Brueghel the Elder was a Renaissance man whose outlook and much of whose subject-matter were still intensely medieval, and whose pictures must still be 'read' in detail.

Brueghel and Chaucer have one point of social background in common. Each worked primarily for a courtly audience. For Chaucer it was the nobility of the age of Richard II, for Brueghel it was the nobility of the great era of Philip II. Brueghel, too, worked within the tradition of the Months of the Year, showing the life of the peasants, but did not intend them to be studied for their own images. Brueghel was also a most impres-sive social critic and a painter with a mind of intense complexity presenting society as no previous artist had done before him. The outcome looks so obvious and so photo-graphic that one accepts it as literal statement.

The first painting showing the labours of July and August (**122**) happens to reveal very few of the peasants at work, scything the corn, binding the sheaves or gathering

122 *The Harvesters.* P. Brueghel

123 *Peasant Wedding*. P. Brueghel

apples. Brueghel has turned his eye upon them at the noontime break when one is
asleep and others are sitting on the sheaves taking their meal. The basket of bread is in
the foreground and a man is making his way towards us with a jug of ale. The peasants
are eating bowls of curds and raw onions. Turning into the distance we can see the
church, the village and the bay beyond. The field in the foreground and the one high
up in the distance is, in the original, yellow with ripe corn, while the fields in the centre
with the hay-wain are greener. Orchards, grazing, and common land are depicted.
The birds overhead, the ladder in the orchard, the sun-hats, all are proof of a most
sympathetic observation of how the individual labourer worked.

The others are more interesting pictures which show holiday and festivity in action.
The Peasant Wedding (123) is dominated by a large table slanting diagonally across the
canvas, with settle, benches and seats; the unhinged door is used as a large tray and
the side-board emphasizes the textural theme of wood. The background, carefully examined, turns out to be a great wall of corn-straw into which a pitchfork has been
stuck to support the cloth, to which has been pinned the crown over the bride's head.
That lady is so plain, smug, and dumpy that it is not entirely surprising that there is no

124 *Peasant Dance*. P. Brueghel

immediate sign of the groom. He may be the young man intently eating with his back to the settle.

A friar is seen talking to a gentleman in black who is something of an enigma. He has been interpreted as Brueghel inserting himself into his own painting, seeing life from the sidelines exactly as Chaucer did as a pilgrim. This is not at all unlikely except that when he mixed among the people to collect visual impressions it is known that he wore less distinctive dress. Lots of other people in the background are dying to burst into the room, but in accordance with a statute of Charles V the company does not exceed twenty guests. The child at the front of the picture with the long peacock feather in her hat is finding compensation for apparent neglect by gormandizing happily. Note the bagpipe-players, and the 'points' or strings which lace up their hose at the waist.

The Peasant Dance (**124**) is less crowded and less inhibited by social convention. The bagpiper and the child reappear. The same impression predominates. Having eaten and drunk, and fallen now to dancing, they are all extremely clumsy as they tread through a rustic measure. Two people embrace, while another couple is coming out of the house to join the dance. Others in the scene are too inebriated to stir, their expression revealing their natures without a trace of sentimentality.

Just as the structure of the barn was carefully delineated in the last painting, so here Brueghel has been most careful to depict the grouping of cottages and fences. On the tree there is a religious picture. Note the man with the motley clothes who turns out to have a fool's cap with ass's ears. He is the medieval fool who is only professionally simple but underneath it all a most wise man. Here, I think, he is the rather remote viewpoint from which the painter is seeing the scene: the fool is his substitute. There is no moralizing and no need for a friar, it is simply a festive picture in which the quality of the life and the merriment is accepted.

Other Brueghel canvases show him as an allegorist and a more fully extended moralist. He takes biblical subjects and popular sayings, he concentrates more upon human nature in child form. In some of his work he seems to show a great bitterness, to be compared more with William Langland than with Geoffrey Chaucer. But it is with Chaucer, Shakespeare and Ben Jonson that Brueghel should be compared. Having seen three paintings the reader is advised to discover still more. The clarity, strength and humanity of his work are immediately striking. Not even a room full of French Impressionists can give so much evidence of felt life and genuine humanity, nor convey so well what it is that the painter can take from and give back to his society. For the writer the room in the Vienna museum from which **123** and **124** come is the high-water mark of European painting of the Middle Ages and Renaissance combined.

To take the general ideas of this book further and without encountering too great a degree of specialization the following books will be of interest:

J. J. Bagley *Life in Medieval England* (Batsford)
Derek Brewer *Chaucer in his Time* (Nelson)
M. Hussey, A. C. Spearing, J. Winny *An Introduction to Chaucer* (Cambridge)
G. M. Trevelyan *English Social History* Illustrated edition, Vol. 1 (Penguin Books)

Among the many books for taking specialized topics further the following may be helpful:

M. D. Anderson *The Imagery of British Churches* (Murray)
M. W. Beresford and J. K. St Joseph *Medieval England: An Aerial Survey* (Cambridge)
Muriel Bowden *A Commentary on the 'General Prologue'* (Macmillan)
Hugh Braun *Introduction to English Medieval Architecture* (Faber and Faber)
W. C. Curry *Chaucer and the Medieval Sciences* (Allen and Unwin)
John Harvey *Gothic England* (Batsford)
Arnold Hauser *Social History of Art* (Routledge)
David Knowles and J. K. St Joseph *Monastic Sites from the Air* (Cambridge)
May McKisack *The Fourteenth Century* (Oxford)
A. R. Myers *England in the Late Middle Ages* (Penguin Books)
A. L. Poole *Medieval England*, 2 vols (Oxford)
Margaret Rickert *Painting in Britain: The Middle Ages* (Penguin Books)
L. F. Salzman *English Trade in the Middle Ages* (Pordes)

In addition to this, many readers may be able to look for the traces of buildings and other remnants of medieval life in different parts of England. Where this is the case, the following list of places may be helpful as a beginning:

London, with Westminster, will naturally recommend itself to every student searching for remnants of medieval life. The illustrations of architecture in this book will have given him an indication of a few other cities to visit. Castles, churches and cathedrals are not to be seen in isolation. The layout of the town-centre, the cobblestones and the twisting paths, are as revealing as pillars and spires.

The visitor will find little of direct relevance to the life of Chaucer. Aldgate and Westminster, where he lived, have altered completely, and so has Cheapside where his father's business was situated. The poet's tomb is in the Poet's Corner in Westminster Abbey. There is little else for which to seek.

Canterbury and York, as the twin pillars of the Church of England, have many

125 *Old Court, Corpus Christi College, Cambridge*

claims upon the traveller's attention: the latter especially when (as in 1969) the York Mystery Cycle of medieval plays is being performed in the Abbey grounds and in the streets on the small pageant wagons, as were originally in use. Apart from these two archiepiscopal sees, all other medieval cathedrals deserve careful attention. Contemporary with the work already discussed at Canterbury was that in progress at both Gloucester and Winchester. At Ely Cathedral the Lady Chapel and the beautiful octagon that crowns the entire building are the work of Chaucer's lifetime. But it is notorious that churches and cathedrals were always being built, destroyed and rebuilt so that there are few large examples that catch the style of a single period. The unique exception is Salisbury Cathedral, where only the tower and the spire were erected after the thirteenth century and where the exterior is one of the finest of all. On the construction of the spire one should read the novel *The Spire* by William Golding (who lives a short distance from the Cathedral). Salisbury is one of the best examples that

England can show of medieval chequer-board planning, since it was built speedily to house a community already gathered on the site of Old Sarum and anxious to remove to less crowded premises.

Southwell Minster in Nottinghamshire, a cathedral in all but name, is a building notable for the perfection of its internal decoration. With all its pillars festooned in stone-carvings of leaves from all manner of trees, interspersed with small animals and acorns and berries, one can see that Gothic builders enjoyed the fantasy of creating a forest out of stone, and that they left it virtually perfect as a tribute to the beauty of the natural world.

The traveller who finds himself in Peterborough should not fail to see Longthorpe Tower, which is the finest example in the country of a domestic building that retains a series of allegorical wall-paintings in good condition. Not far from here the traveller should consider the wool churches of East Anglia, such as those of Long Melford and Lavenham. These great churches are the most lasting tribute we have to the economic advantages of sheep-rearing, since they resulted in churches far too large for the local population but built spacious and high for the glory of God.

All over England and Wales the visitor will see castles which have remained in a good state of preservation because of the exceptional solidity of their construction. Beaumaris and Pembroke, Hurstmonceux (now the Royal Observatory) in Sussex, Warwick, Carisbrooke, and Kenilworth, the home of John of Gaunt, are notable. Nor should medieval bridges be overlooked since they were the responsibility of different gilds who kept them in good repair. Huntingdon, Lostwithiel in Cornwall, Eamont in Cumberland and St Ives in Huntingdonshire are a few which will give the same idea of solidity that is to be felt in castles and in the earliest cathedrals—the solidity of buildings meant for posterity.

The universities of Oxford and Cambridge are naturally included in any historical itinerary, although they do not contain a great deal of their original buildings. The cloister at New College has been illustrated: there are similar cloisters at Magdalen and Merton Colleges, while in Cambridge the cloister-pattern is not quite so prominent. The fortified gatehouse, as at Queens', Trinity and St John's Colleges, may be more typical. The oldest parts of Cambridge University are at Peterhouse, Pembroke and Corpus Christi. The last preserves in its Old Court the most complete range of medieval college buildings, with the passageway to St Bene't's Church, from which the college formerly took its name (**125**).

If one looks for further examples of paintings and smaller works, the cathedrals of Exeter and Norwich are especially rich in roof bosses. In the Bauchun Chapel in Norwich will be found a series of bosses based on the same theme as the *Man of Law's Tale* (of which there is no suitable reproduction). The altar-painting known as the

Norwich Retable, one of the best preserved of fourteenth-century examples, is an important addition to the history of medieval English art.

There is a great deal of medieval material all over the rest of England and many more books written as guides to it. Although most of the parish churches were completed before Chaucer's birth, the last half of the fourteenth century was still a productive period in medieval art. The reign of Richard II that brought it to a close was richer than any until the time of Queen Elizabeth, when it was the turn of the smaller country-house rather than the castle to be added to the scenery as the monasteries were destroyed or converted to other uses. But none of the other medieval arts has more power to attract modern adherents than the literary ones, so that those unable to visit the sites of a castle, a cathedral or a college are in no sense deprived of direct contact with the finest of medieval forms of expression. It has been the purpose of the present book to suggest that the all-connecting centre of English medieval life is its literature.

LIST OF ILLUSTRATIONS

Frontispiece. Canterbury Cathedral   *page*   2

1   A Fourteenth-century Map of England: the Gough Map   8

2   Chaucer's England: a Modern Map showing all the Place-names mentioned
     by Chaucer, and other Sites mentioned in this Book   10

3   Chaucer's Europe: a Modern Map showing all the Place-names mentioned
     by Chaucer   12

4   A diagram of the Pilgrim's Way   14

5   An old Plan of Canterbury   16

6   The Martyrdom of St Thomas à Becket: a Roof boss   18

7   Months of the Year   20
     a *January, drinking by the fire*
     b *February, digging in the fields and setting seed*
     c *March, pruning vines*
     d *April, carrying flowering branch*
     e *May, hawking*
     f *June, mowing the hay*
     g *July, cutting the corn with a sickle*
     h *August, threshing with a flail*
     i *September, picking grapes*
     j *October, sowing winter corn*
     k *November, gathering acorns to feed the pigs*
     l *December, pig-killing*

8   Signs of the Zodiac   23
     a *Aquarius, the water-carrier*
     b *Pisces, the fishes*
     c *Aries, the ram*
     d *Taurus, the bull*
     e *Gemini, the twins*
     f *Cancer, the crab*
     g *Leo, the lion*
     h *Virgo, the virgin*
     i *Libra, the balance*
     j *Scorpio, the scorpion*
     k *Sagittarius, the archer*
     l *Capricorn, the goat*

9   The Three Estates   24

10	A Group of Fifteenth-century Pilgrims	25
11	Pilgrims leaving Southwark from the Tabard Inn	26
12	The George Inn, Glastonbury	27
13	Great Gidding	31
14	Padbury	32
15	Braunton	33
16	Fourteenth-century Cottage in Hagbourne, Berkshire	34
17	Fourteenth-century Cottage in Didbrook, Gloucestershire	35
18	The Knight	37
19	Sir Geoffrey Luttrell in Armour	38
20	Storming a Castle	39
21	Riding with the King	40
22	Jousting	41
23	Stokesay Castle	42
24	Old Sarum	43
25	Warkworth Castle	44
26	Caernarvon Castle	45
27	Seventeenth-century Plan of Caernarvon	46
28	Bodiam Castle	47
29	The Squire	48
30	The Month of May. *Pol de Limbourg*	49
31a	Musicians and their Instruments	50
31b	Musicians and their Instruments	50
32	'Fine Amour' (Romantic Love)	51
33	The Month of December: a Boar-hunt. *Pol de Limbourg*	53
34	The Prioress	55
35	The Second Nun	55
36	Convent Life	56
37	The Monk	57
38	The Monk in his Cell	58
39	Illuminated MS: the Lord's Prayer	60
40	Illuminated MS: a Page from the Luttrell Psalter	62
41	The 'Queene of Fortune'	63
42	Ground-plan of Fountains Abbey	65
43	Fountains Abbey	66
44	New College, Oxford	68

45 The Friar   70
46 Preaching   71
47 The Merchant   72
48 Entry in Gilbert Maghfield's Day Book 'Geoffrey Chaucer owes 28s. 6d from
    26 July until the following Saturday'   73
49 London from the Tower   74
50 The Merchant, Januarie, and the Young Wife, May   75
51 The Clerk   76
52 The University Lecture   76
53 Illustrations from *Margarita Philosophica*
    a *Grammar*   78
    b *The Institution of Hebrew and Greek*   79
    c *Rhetoric*   80
    d *Logic*   81
    e *Music*   82
    f *Arithmetic*   83
    g *Geometry*   83
    h *Astronomy*   84
    i *Philosophy*   85
54 A Medieval Bookseller   86
55 The Sergeant of the Law   87
56 The King's Bench Court in the Fifteenth Century   88
57 The Chancery Court in the Fifteenth Century   89
58 The Franklin   90
59 The Dangers of Self-indulgence   91
60 The Manciple   92
61 The Hall, Lincoln's Inn   93
62 The *Taille*, or Tally Stick   94
63 The Warden of a Gild with two Craftsmen   95
64 The Merchant Venturers Guildhall, York   96
65 The Cook   97
66a Cooking Operations   98
66b Cooking Operations   98
67 The Shipman   99
68 Ships at Anchor   100
69 Dartmouth   101
70 The Doctor of Physic   102

71   The Zodiac Man   103
72   The four Humours   104
73   Manipulative Surgery   107
74   The Black Death leaves its Mark   109
75   The Wife of Bath   110
76   The Wife beating her Husband (Misericord in Carlisle Cathedral)   111
77   Venus and her Children   112
78   Mars and his Children   113
79   The Wheel of the Senses   115
80   The Parson   116
81   A Medieval Parish Church (Hanwell, Oxfordshire)   117
82   St Christopher (a Mural)   118
83   A 'Doom' Painting   119
84   A Seven Sacrament Window   121
85   Pride   123
86   Covetousness   123
87   Lechery with Chastity   124
88   Anger   125
89   Gluttony with Abstinence   126
90   Envy with Charity   126
91   Sloth   127
92   Grotesque from Lincoln Cathedral   127
93   Ploughing   128
94   The Peasants' Revolt   130
95   The Miller   131
96   A Water-mill   132
97   A Bagpiper   132
98   The Reeve   133
99   The Reeve in the Field   133
100 Saturn and his Children   134
101 'The sheep hath paid for all'   135
102 The Summoner   136
103 Hell. *Pol de Limbourg*   137
104 The Pardoner   138
105 Death calls for the Bishop   140
106 A Tomb and Cadaver   141

107 The Nun's Priest   142
108 February. *Pol de Limbourg*   143
109 The Fox preaching   145
110 The Dog-piper   146
111 The Goat   146
112 The Donkey   147
113 The Corpse   147
114 The Canon's Yeoman   148
115 The Alchemist's Laboratory   149
116 Mercury and his Children   150
117 Cosmological Scene   152
118 Chaucer   154
119 Chaucer's Autograph   154
120 John of Gaunt   155
121 The Wilton Diptych   159
122 The Harvesters. *Pieter Brueghel*   160
123 Peasant Wedding. *Pieter Brueghel*   161
124 Peasant Dance. *Pieter Brueghel*   162
125 Old Court, Corpus Christi College, Cambridge   165